AF662868

Letters of

Hadrat Abu Bakr Siddiq (R.A.A.)

Letters of
Hadrat Abu Bakr Siddiq
(R.A.A.)

Translated by
Dr. Hafiz Muhammad Adil
M.A., LL.B., Ph.D.

KITAB BHAVAN
New Delhi-2 [India]

KITAB BHAVAN
Publishers, Distributors, Exporters & Importers
1784, Kalan Mahal, Darya Ganj,
New Delhi - 1100 02 (India)

Phones : (91-11) 23277392/93, 23274686, 32906494
Fax : (91-11) 23263383
Website : www.kitabbhavan.com
Email : nasri@vsnl.com
: nusrat@bol.net.in

2rd Edition 2009

ISBN : 81-7151-203-8
Book Code No. : L00060

Laser Typesetting at:
Laser Track
1784, Kalan Mahal, Darya Ganj
New Delhi - 1100 02 [India]

Printed & Published in India by :
Nusrat Ali Nasri for KITAB BHAVAN
1784, Kalan Mahal, Darya Ganj,
New Delhi - 1100 02 [India]

LETTERS OF HADRAT ABU BAKR SIDDIQ (R.A.A.)

CONTENTS

INTRODUCTION vi

(1) To All The Rebel Tribes 1

(2) Directive to The Army is Commanders 4

(3) Directive to Khalid Bin Waleed (R.A.A.) 6

DESPATCHES ADDRESSED TO KHALID BIN WALEED (R.A.A.) 9

(4) Letter 10

(5) Letter 11

(6) Letter To 'Ikrima Bin Abi Jehl (R.A.A.) 12

(7) Another Version of The Letter 13

(8) To Shuraihbeel-Bin-Hasana (R.A.A.) 13

(9) To Khalid Bin Waleed (R.A.A.) 14

The Reply of Khalid Bin Waleed (R.A.A.) 19

From Khalid Bin Waleed (R.A.A.) 21

(10) To Khalid Bin Waleed (R.A.A.) 21

(11) To Khalid Bin Waleed (R.A.A.) 22

(12) To Turaifa Bin Hajiz 23

(13) To Khalid Bin Waleed (R.A.A.) 25

(14) To 'Amr Bin Al-'Aas (R.A.A.) And Waleed Bin 'Uqbah 26

REBELLION IN YAMAN 28

(15) To Yamani Chiefs 30

(16) To Tahir Bin Abi Hala 30

(17) To 'At-Taab Bin Usaid (R.A.A.) 31

(18) Addressed to Muhajir Bin Umayya 32

(19) Document Given to The Christians of Najran 34

REBELLION IN BAHRAIN 35

(20) To 'Ala Bin Hadhrami (R.A.A.) 35

(21) Addressed to Anas Bin Malik (R.A.A.) 36

REBELLION IN AMMAN 39

(22) To 'Amr Bin Al 'Aas (R.A.A.) 39

(23) To 'Ikrima Bin Abi Jehl 40

REBELLION IN HADRAMAUT AND KINDA 43

(24) Addressed to Ziyad Bin Lubaid Ansari (R.A.A.) 43

(25) Addressed To Ash'as Bin Qais And Another Chief of Banu Kinda 44

(26) To 'Ikrima Bin Abi Jehl 46

(27) To Muhajir Bin Abi Umayyah 49

(28) To Muhajir Bin Abi Umayyah 50

(29) To Muhajir Bin Abi Umayyah 50

(30) To The Commanders of The Area of Apostates 51

(31) To Khalid Bin Waleed (R.A.A.) 52

CONQUEST OF IRAQ 53

(32) To Khalid Bin Waleed (R.A.A.) 53

(33) To 'Iyaz Bin Ghanam 54

(34) To Khalid Bin Waleed And 'Iyaz Bin Ghanam 54

(35) To Khalid Bin Waleed (R.A.A.) And 'Iyaz Bin Ghanam 55

(36) To Khalid Bin Waleed And 'Iyaz Bin Ghanam (R.A.A.) 55

(37) To Khalid Bin Waleed (R.A.A.) And His Forces 56

(38) To Maz'ur Bin 'Adi 58

(39) Letter 59

	CONQUESTS IN SYRIA	60
(40)	To The Muslims of Yaman	61
(41)	To Khalid Bin Saeed	62
(42)	Letter	63
(43)	Letter	63
(44)	To 'Amr Bin Al-'Aas	63
(45)	To 'Amr Bin Al-'Aas	64
(46)	Letter	65
(47)	To All The Military Commanders	66
(48)	To 'Amr Bin Al-'Aas (R.A.A.)	66
(49)	Letter	67
(50)	To The Military Commanders	67
(51)	To Khalid Bin Waleed (R.A.A.)	68
	POLICY DIRECTIVES TO THE MILITARY COMMANDERS	69
	LETTERS TO COMMANDERS IN SYRIA	73
(52)	Reply to Abu Obaidah Bin Jarrah (R.A.A.)	75
(53)	Reply to Yazid Bin Abi Sufyan (R.A.A.)	75
(54)	To Abu Obaidah Bin Jarrah (R.A.A.)	77
(55)	To Khalid Bin Waleed (R.A.A.)	79
(56)	To Abu Ohaidah Bin Jarrah (R.A.A.)	80
	FROM KHALID BIN WALEED (R.A.A.) TO ABU OBAIDAH BIN JARRAII (R.A.A.)	82
(57)	To The Commanders of The Army	82
	Proclamation To Succession	84

Introduction

After the Holy Prophet Muhammad (S.A.W.), Hadrat Abu Bakr Siddiq (R.A.A.) is the most dignified, outstanding and reverred personality among the Muslims. It is indeed a great honour and privilege, for a person like me, to translate the letters and despatches of such an august personality. It is merely a good luck that the publisher, Mr. Akhlaq Hussain, selected, me for such a noble task, and as such I am grateful to him for this honour shown to me.

The Publisher has already published the letters of the Holy Prophet (S.A.W.) in English. Now, this is the second book of the series, containing the letters of the First Caliph of Islam. Compilation and translation of the letters of other Caliphs is in hand.

I have tried my best to translate the letters as faithfully as possible, and have avoided the deviation from the original text. If any reader of this book finds any error or deviation, and points it out to me through the Publisher, I will gratefully acknowledge it, and correct it in the next edition. While translating, I came across a great difficulty. Several versions of a single letter were found in many books. Some were quoted briefly, some moderately and some as detailed as possible, but inviting the doubts about its authenticity. I have selected only those letters which are fairly detailed and comprehensive but simultaneously authentic. Only those short letters have been included which present something new.

Now a few words about the quality and style of the letters.

The letters written by the first Caliph of the Prophet (S.A.W.) are pithy, brief, short and to the point. They are written in a very simple, factual, realistic and forceful language, avoiding rhetoric, verbosity and superfluity. They are impressive, convincing and appealing to the common sense direct as if heart to heart talk. These letters are administrative in nature. They were written due to political expediency and to carry the mission entrusted to Hadrat Abu Bakr (R.A.A.). His was the most critical period in the history of Islam. An iron hand with firm determination to deal with the situation was the pressing need of the hour. Three anti-forces were working against Islam at that time:

(1) Withholding the payment of Zakat,

(2) Apostasy movement in Arabia, and

(3) The false claimants to prophethood.

The addressees were invited to give up what was wrong, and to accept the right, the true way of Islam. These administrative despatches clearly manifest profound truthfulness, honesty, firmness, keeping up the promises and final and firm conviction in the ultimate success. These despatches deeply impress the heart, head and the hand. They infuse the idea of the presence of a hard-task master with a loving disposition who can show no leniency in discharging his duties as the first lieutenant of the Prophet of Allah (S.A.W.).

The main features of these despatches are:

(1) The despatches addressed to different commanders of the army of Islam invariably begin with *"(Bismillah-hir-Rahman-nir-Raheem.)" (In* the name of Allah, The Compassionate, the Merciful).

(2) The letters indicate that these were from the Caliph or successor of the Prophet of Allah, Muhammad (S.A.W.).

(3) Thereafter, the name or names of the addressees, along with their surnames appear.

(4) The letters open with a sentence either in the praise of Allah or an invocation of His Mercy.

(5) Then follows the subject matter of the letters, especially administrative in nature: The sentences are brief, to the point, forceful and highly cultured.

From the study of the despatches of Caliph Abu Bakr (R.A.A.), it is crystal clear that they are a practical demonstration of the utmost endeavour to keep up, maintain, intensify and finally to establish the system of life — *Deen* — as propounded by the Holy Prophet Muhammad (S.A.W.). Caliph Abu Bakr left no stone unturned in carrying out the behests of his beloved master (S.A.W.) in letter and spirit as he was the most intimate person knowing fully well the working theory of the Prophet of Islam (S.A.W.).

As can be seen through the pages of history, in a few years after Hijrat, the Prophet of Allah (S.A.W.) carried the message of Islam in the far off distant corners of Arabian Peninsula, and thus laid the foundation of Islamic State as enunciated in Quran Majeed. The establishment of the infant state at Madina was a living practical demonstration of the Quranic theory of life. It will not be out of place to mention that the Prophet of Allah (S.A.W.) breathed his last when the process of intellectual awakening was at the initial stage. The demise of Prophet of Allah (S.A.W.) seemed to be the bursting of the lava from a volcano. A considerable populace of Arabia became hostile to the newly established deen-Islam as it had not gone deep into the very core of their hearts. The old habits, forming part of their second nature, were being revived. A section of the people of Arabia turned apostate, withheld payment of Zakat. The tax collectors of the Prophet of Allah (S.A.W.) and the teachers well-versed in the Quranic teachings left their respective headquarters and returned to Madina. As already stated the main reasons for the apostasy movement after the demise of the Prophet of Allah (S.A.W.) were.

(a) General deviation from the collective responsibilities and moral obligations of Islam,

(b) Withholding the payment of Zakat.

(c) General disliking of the tribal chiefs because of the decrease in their power due to the effective control from the Centre, Madina.

So there were three main opponents—in Yaman Aswad 'Ansi, Musailimah in Yamamah and Tulaiha in Najd. Aswad 'Ansi met his fate earlier, his career came to an early end as seen through the despatches of the Caliph Abu Bakr (R.A.A.) The other two gained timely power to be overthrown subsequently as seen from the letters. The tribesmen of Musailimah, more than forty thousand in number, had gathered in Yamamah and other strongholds. Yamamah was the most prosperous city after Mecca and Madina. The power of Tulaiha increased alarmingly round the capital of Islam as several tribes men turned rebels, joined the enemy, and the danger was hovering over Madina.

On the 12th Rabi-ul-Awwal, 11 A.H. Abu Bakr (R.A.A.) was elected the caliph of the Messenger of Allah (S.A.W.), certainly against his wishes. The situation was extremely critical. There was potent danger to the newly established ideological infant state of Madina.

A few of the outstanding companions of the Prophet of Allah (S.A.W.) expressed their disapproval and resentment over the newly elected Caliph Abu Bakr (R.A.A.); the hypocrites in Madina were happy to see that the newly established state of Islam is coming to an end, the main source of income Zakat had been withheld. It appeared that the Caliphate of the Messenger of Allah (S.A.W.) had been encircled in a whirlpool of trials and turmoils.

Almighty Allah helped the believing Muslims to stabilise the infant Muslim State of Madina and the personality of Abu Bakr (R.A.A.) was brought in the lime light. He seemed to be a man of iron-nerves now, though his heart was aglow with his merciful disposition. The impending dangers, difficulties enumerated above sat very lightly upon his mind. It was characteristic of him to show greater resoluteness and determination according to the degree of danger and impending perils. Constant company of the Prophet of Allah (S.A.W.) and consequent love for Islam engendered in him wonderful power of confidence amounting to certitude, equanimity of conduct, excellence of character and forbearance against the counsel of many influential and important persons of the state. Soon after becoming the Caliph or the true lieutenant of the Messenger of Allah (S.A.W.), Abu Bakr (R.A.A.) delivered the following *Khutba* (inaugural address) to the public as well as to the elite. It is a landmark in the history of the Caliphate of Islam. The address was in the following strain after the usual Islamic way of praise due to Almighty Allah and the benedictions and blessings to the Holy Prophet (S.A.W.):

"O people! I have been elected as your Ameer (chief) and Wali (Administrator) but I am not in any way superior to you. If I act in the right direction, help me, but if I deviate, put me to the right path. Be it known to all that truth is truth, while falsehood is sheer dishonesty. Remember, that the weak among you is strong before me till I restore his, due right, God willing, and the strong among you is powerless before me, till I take away the due right belonging to others, Insha Allah. The nation that relinquishes Jehad, surely that will meet its fate of degradation before Allah. The Ummah (nation) addicted to shameless activities is put to toil and tribulations by Almighty Allah. As long as I obey Almighty Allah and the Messenger of Allah (S.A.W.) you obey me. Be ready for the prayers. Allah will show mercy upon you."

(The above address is based upon the narration of Anas bin Malik (R.A.A.) as stated by Muhammad bin Ishaque bin Yasar.).

The inaugural address is noted for its being succinct, pithy, brief, to the point, minimum words to express the maximum, all embracing and comprehensive. In the first instance it reflects the basic theory of administration in Islam that all are equal in the eyes of law, that all enjoy freedom of conscience and speech, that the Caliph Abu Bakr (R.A.A.) is subject to criticism to enable him to tread the right path. These words were spoken in those days when Qaiser and Kisra enjoyed unlimited powers. Their word was law and they were themselves above law. Even today in British Constitution the king can do no wrong. Truth but truth was the main stay of the life of the first caliph of prophet of Allah (S.A.W.). Again vindication of the rights of the weak was the personal responsibility of the Caliph, and those rights were to be seized from those whosoever strong. Again the basic need to survive in Islam is Jehad, to strive in the way of Allah, the Supreme with ones own health, and wealth, irrespective of all considerations—the main objective being to establish the supremacy and preponderance of the laws of Allah, the Great brought by His Messenger (S.A.W.). If the Caliph did not conform to the above ideological theory of State — obedience to Allah and His Messenger (S.A.W.), the Caliph is not to be obeyed. It is not incumbent upon the people to obey him if he does not himself obey the commands of Allah and His Messenger (S.A.W.).

In short, if the above address of the first Caliph of Islam be put to practice in modern times, it can be a harbinger of a new era of happiness and social justice where Machiavellian philosophy of politics prevails in practice—forgery is not forgery, crime is no crime, theft is no theft, if it is committed in the interest of the State. The despatches of the first Caliph of Islam (R.A.A.) to various commanders of the first Muslim State with headquarters at Madina exhort that they are duty bound by Omnipresent Allah to keep up their words, not to molest the women, the feeble and the old, the infirm, not to cut trees while on March, not to send chopped off heads of the enemy but despatches in news are sufficient; are a tower of light when compared with the contemporary behaviour of the European, Persian and Roman emperors. The clean state policy adopted by Caliph Abu Bakr (R.A.A.) as seen through his letters can solve all the problems of present Muslims, if a single minded personality like him comes forward and performs his duty with courage, determination and integrity like the first Caliph of the Messenger of Allah (S.A.W.). May Almighty Allah grant us a personality who may prove a true follower and successor of the first lieutenant of the Messenger of Allah (S.A.W.).

Our actions are dependant upon the guidance of Allah. Ameen !

In the end, it may safely be stated that Hadrat Abu Bakr (R.A.A.) rightly got the appellation of SIDDIQUE i.e. the Truthful. It may be designated as a supreme quality of a Muslim. Truthfulness is a very comprehensive term and bears the widest scope. It is coterminus with life. Imam Ghazali has enumerated the following six qualities of gradations of a true Muslim. (a) True in words; (b) Ture in intention and will; (c) True in resoluteness of determination; (d) True in the completion of determination, (e) True in action and (f) Ture in all stages of his religion. From his writings it is evident that the above qualities reflect themselves from his speeches, addresses and despatches. So, truthfulness was his diplomacy — the most maligned word used in modern politics—through which the first Caliph Abu Bakr (R.A.A.) managed international affairs by negotiations. It is the method by which relations are adjusted and managed by ambassadors and envoys. So, truth was his business or art as a diplomat. May Allah shower his benedictions upon this first and the most intimate lieutenant of His Messenger, Muhammad (S.A.W.) Ameen!

True in words and true in deeds — indeed!

LETTERS OF HADRAT ABU BAKR SIDDIQ (R.A.A.)

(1)

TO ALL THE REBEL TRIBES

In the name of Allah — All compassionate and Most Merciful

"From the Caliph of the Prophet of Allah, Abu Bakr, to the Elite and the public whether they believe in Islam or turned apostate peace be upon them who are firm on the right and peaceful path of Islam and did not deviate towards the wrong way. I bear witness that there is none worthy of worship except Allah, who is Unique and without any Partner, declare that Muhammad (S.A.W.) is His Servant and Messenger, and further affirm and believe in the trustworthiness and truthfulness of the message brought by him. Those who do not accept his message, I declare that they are nonbelievers (Kafirs) and am constantly in a state of war with them. Let it be made clear that Allah sent the Messenger of Islam (S.A.W.) with true revelation and teachings, as the Caller towards Allah, messenger of good tidings, a warner and a bright lamp of guidance, so that the Prophet of Allah (S.A.W.) warn human beings against evil and be a perfect argument against the kafirs (non-believers).

"To warn whosoever liveth, and that the word may be fulfilled against the disbelievers."

(Al-Quran) 36;70).

Those who accepted the message of the Prophet of Allah, Muhammad (S.A.W.), God guided them on the right path, those who deviated from it, they were punished by the Messenger of

Allah till they became Muslim. After some time, when the Messenger of God (S.A.W.) proclaimed, executed His command, completed his mission, and fulfilled his responsibilities in the welfare of his people, the Prophet of Allah breathed his last — the news of his demise was already given by God in the revealed Book.

> "You are to die and all of them shall die. No one was allowed a perpetual life before you. If you die, can they live for ever. We appointed immortality for no mortal before thee. What! If thou diest, can they be immortal."
>
> *(Al-Quran,* 21: 34)

Allah says:

> "Muhammad (S.A.W.) is but a messenger, messengers (the like of whom) have passed away before him. Will it he that, when he dieth or is slain, ye will turn back on your heels? He who turneth back doth no hurt to Allah, and Allah will reward the thankful." (3.144)

Whoso worships Muhammad (S.A.W.), be it known to him that Muhammad (S.A.W.), has passed away and whoso worships Allah, the Unique, without any partner, he should know that he is under the observation of Allah the Living, Existing on his own, Perpetual, neither slumber nor sleep overtakes Him Who is aware of His every action and punishes the disobedient.

O People! I enjoin upon you to fear God, and be worthy of the good luck and reward that Allah wishes to bestow upon you, and act according to the mode of life that your Prophet (S.A.W.) has brought for you, and follow the path shown by him, and hold steadfast the Deen of Allah (way of Life as ordained by Allah through His Prophet Muhammad (S.A.W.) because whomsoever He guided not, is a deluded one, and whomsoever He cures not from the ailments of defective thinking and consequent wrong in sight is a sick person. He is always looked down upon who has not received the guidance of Allah. Allah says that the person will receive guidance whom Allah Wills; whomsoever is deluded by Him (because of his intransigence, neither will get a helper nor a guide, none of his deeds will be acceptable to God because of his disbelief in this world and will not be compensated in the hereafter as he does not believe in Allah.

The news about those who have accepted Islam, and deviated from it after acting upon it, has been received by me. This deviation is due to the fact that they are in disillusionment about the Power of God and His Punishment because truly they do not realise them. Besides, the Satan has also misguided them. Allah, the Praiseworthy, says,

> "And (remember) when We said unto the angels: Fall prostrate before Adam, and they fell prostrate all save Iblis. He was of the Jinn, so he rebelled against his Lord's Command. Will ye choose him and his seed for your protecting friends instead of Me, when they are enemy unto you? Calamitous is the exchange for evildoers!"
>
> *(Al-Quran,* 18.50).

In another place, Allah, the Exalted, says:

> "Lo! the devil is an enemy for you, so treat him as an enemy. He only summoneth his faction to be owners of the flaming Fire."
>
> *(Al-Quran,* 35:6).

I am sending a person along with an army of *taa-bi-'een* (companions of the companions) of the Prophet of Allah (S.A.W.), Ansar (Helpers of Medina) and Muhaajireen (the emigrants of Mecca), who has been commanded by me not to kill a person or fight with anyone until and unless called upon to recite the Kalimah-i-Shahaadat i.e. I stand to witness that there is not god except Allah and Muhammad is His Messenger

(S.A.W.) Whosoever accepts this, affirms the same, promises to shun sin, and do the virtuous actions, his Islam (return to Deen) may be accepted and also be helped to be steadfast in it and the good deeds. But those who deny to recite the Kalimah or recitation to stand witness that there is no god except Allah I have ordered the Commander-in-Chief of the Army to fight with them, not to show any clemency to those over whom he may obtain power, they should be burnt in fire, killed in every possible manner, their women folk, children and the old persons should be taken as slaves. He should not talk to any one except in terms of recitation of the Kalimah mentioned above and consequent return to Islam—their return to Islam will be in their own interest and whoso does not accept Islam, he can never bring any harm to Allah."

(Tarikh Tabari, Vol. 3 PP. 226-227) and *Subh-al-a'shee Qalaqshandi*, Egypt, Vol. 6 P. 384)

NOTE. The above mentioned letter is also found repeated with minor deviations in *Al-Ik-ti faa bimaa tudhammanah mim mughazee Rasool-ullaahi wa mughaazi-ul- khulafa* compiled by Abu Rabe'e Sulaiman Kal-laa-ee balan-si, handwritten M.S. No. 527, Cairo Library, Egypt P. 245.

(2)

DIRECTIVE TO THE ARMY COMMANDERS

In the name of Allah, All Compassionate and Most Merciful.

This is a directive from the Caliph (representative of the Messenger of Allah (S.A.W.), Abu Bakr, to that person who had been commissioned to fight against the apostates. He is directed to be fearful of the Existence of God in all his activities whether secret or open. He is ordered to work wholeheartedly for the preponderance of Islam, really chastize those who turned away from the Right path and are harbouring satanic desires in their hearts. But before actual punishment is accorded, they should be given a chance to recite the *Kalimah Shahadat*. If they accept this call, no action should be taken against them. But if they do not accept this Call, the Commander of the Faithful should fall upon them on every side till they affirm to be Muslims and then they should be given to understand what are their rights and duties as Muslims. They should be dealt with according to the limits of Allah in the matter of give and take i.e. giving their share in the booty coming from Jihad and taking the due share of Zakat. He should not tolerate delay of any kind in this regard, and also not to prevent Muslims to fight against their enemies. After the fighting is over, those who declare to be Muslims, he should recognize them as such and help them in remaining steadfast in Islam. He should remember very well that he is fighting against the rebels of God till they accept and affirm the teachings revealed from. Allah. The moment they accept this and recite the *Kalimah Shahadat* mentioned above, there will be no justification for any action against them. And if anyone does not believe from the bottom of his heart, he will be reckoned by Almighty Allah Himself. Those, who do not recite the *Kalimah Shahadat* will be chased and challenged. Nothing will be acceptable except Islam, Whoso declares his acceptance in Islam and affirms it from the heart, the Commander will accept him as such, will train him in the Islamic Teachings. Those who refuse to accept Islam, the Commander of the faithful will fight against them and if God gives him power over them, he will destroy them by means of weapons and fire. After this, one-fifth of the booty will be kept aside, and the rest will be distributed among the soldiers, and the *khums* (one-fifth) reserved will be sent to us. The Commander is directed to keep the Muslims away from unnecessary haste and plunder; should not allow the Arabs of low status (character) to join the Army lest they may be spies and the Muslims may be harmed on account of their machinations. He is further directed to treat the Muslims nicely, both in march and camp, look after them properly, the forefront and the hinder positions of the army should not be kept too far away. The Muslims should be persuaded to love one another, show tolerance to each other and talk politely."

(Saff Bin Umar, Asadi Vol. III, P. 227)

(3)

DIRECTIVE TO KHALID BIN WALEED (R.A.A.)

(The above mentioned despatch is based on the narration of Saif bin Umar reported in Tarikh Tabari, who had written a complete volume on the rebellion of rad-dah (the apostates) which has since been lost but Tabari has quoted selected extracts, in his book. According to Saifbin-Umar's narration, the first Caliph of the Prophet of Allah, Hadrat Abu Bakr (R.A.A.) had opened eleven fronts for the chastizement of the apostates, appointed a commander of the army for each front to deal with, every commander was provided with two letters, one for the Arab tribesmen and the other for the commander himself for guidance. In Cairo, the Library of Egypt, there are valuable manuscripts in the name of Iktifa dealing with the various expeditions and conquests of the period but no mention has been made of the eleven fronts, nor the eleven commanders. According to Iktifa the first Caliph directed his attention towards Tulaiha and Musailimah in the first instance and put all his energies against them. For this expedition Khalid-BinWaleed (R.A.A.) was appointed as the Supreme Commander and was provided with two kinds of orders — one guiding letter for himself and the other for the Arah tribesmen— the letter has already been produced above and the first one — the guiding force, is as under).

In the name of Allah, All-Compassionate and Most Merciful

These are the directives from the first Caliph of the Prophet of Allah (S.A.W.), Abu Bakr (R.A.A.) to Khalid-binWalid (R.A.A.) who had been commanded to fight against those who had turned away from Islam after the demise of the Prophet of Allah (S.A.W.). Khalid (R.A.A.) is advised to fear God in all his affairs, secret or open; ordered to do his all for the preponderance of Islam, chase and chastize those who have become apostates, and are entertaining devilish designs in their hearts. He is commanded to provide an opportunity to the rebels to realize their evil designs before they are punished, i.e. to recall them to Islam. Those who accept the Call, whether black or white, their Islam should be accepted, they should be treated well but if they do not accept, sword should be used against them. He is on war footing with those only who have denied the Existence of God instead of believing in Him. Those who accept Islam (only by means of tongue) outwardly, no action should be taken against them because their accountability rests in the hands of God. Khalid (R.A.A.) is directed to execute his mission wholeheartedly. The rebels, who do not affirm in Kalimah Shahadat, Khalid (R.A.A.) is ordered to fight against them with the help of Muhajirs and Ansar wherever they may be or whatever place they may run away, whoso falls into the hands of the believers, they should be put to death, and none of them should be spared except on their declaration and recitation that there is none to be worshipped except Allah and Muhammad is His Servant and Messenger. He is further directed to proceed towards Yamamah, fight with their false claiments, Musailimah and Banu Hanifa but before actual fight they should be recalled to Islam, and sincere efforts should be made to bring them back to Islam. If they accept Islam by reciting the *Kalimah Shahadah*, it should be accepted as such, I should be informed of it and should remain in Yamamah till my next directive reaches them. If Banu Hanifa do no accept Islam, do not turn away from infidelity and the following of Musailimah, the liar, Khalid (R.A.A.) is commanded by the Caliph of faithful to fight against them himself and with other Muslims. This is sure that Allah will help Islam and it will dominate over all other religions as has been said in Quran Majeed, however, distasteful let may seem to the unbelievers. If by the Grace of God, Khalid (R.A.A.) is victorious against Banu Hanifa, they should be destroyed with the help of fire and sword. None of them should be spared who can be killed. The booty and their wealth should be distributed among the Muslims after keeping aside one-fifth which should be remitted to me so that I may dispose it off according to Islamic Law.

Khalid (R.A.A.) is directed to keep away his companions from any possible (dissensions,) differences that may weaken them and desist to take action in haste. He is further required not to recruit the low-character Arabs in the Army till their whereabouts and ancestory is ascertained as to what are their beliefs and why they want to fight along with the Muslims. I apprehend that such Arabs may not take refuge in the Muslim Army, who are neither Muslims nor your friends but whose sole aim is to spy the activities of the Muslims. I have this apprehension against the Beduins and the ignorants. In view of this, people of such type should never enter your army. Under all circumstances, whether in camp or the march, treat the Muslims nicely, look after them properly, neither keep away too far one portion of the army from the other one, nor despatch one part of the army before the other one (that may create misunderstanding). Persuade your companions to be good to those Ansar Companions who are in your army; treat them well because they are grief-stricken and disheartened; theirs' is a definite right in Islam, they possess great and good qualities, have rendered yeoman services to the cause of Islam, and above all, they have been recommended by the Messenger of Allah (S.A.W.). So listen to those among them who are victims and connive at those who are mistaken as redirected by the Prophet of Allah (S.A.W.).

DESPATCHES ADDRESSED TO KHALID BIN WALEED (R.A.A.)

NOTE : When Hadrat Abu Bakr (R.A.A.) opened eleven fronts in *Zawil-qas-sab*, the first and the foremost was against Tulaiha and his allies. Khalid Bin Walid (R.A.A.) was appointed as its Commander-in-Chief. He had been ordered to proceed against Tayy, then the Confederates of Tulaiha and lastly march to Butaah, invite Tulaiha to Islam, afterwards bring Malik bin Nuwaira to the Right Path, and murderers of Muslims who had been burnt by the different tribesmen should be demanded and put to death. At this time, Tulaiha was encamped in his locality near the tank of Buzakha along with powerful tribes of Ghatfan, Tayy, Fazara, Jadila, 'A-bas and Zubyan. According to the instructions of the Caliph, Khalid (R.A.A.) marched against the tribe of Tayy, whose villages were situated in the middle of mountains, about fifty miles in the North West of Madina. The son of Hatim of Tayy, 'Adi, a sincere Muslim, intelligent, influential head of his tribe, worked with such sagacity that his tribe of Tayy got out of the Confederation of Tulaiha, and another powerful clan of Jadila also separated itself along with their 1000 men from Tulaiha. Tulaiha remained in Buzakha along with his tribe of Banu Asad and his other confederates of the tribes of 'Abas, Zubyan and Ghatfan. Even then he and his allies were in high spirits, Muslims and the renegades arrayed themselves in the battle-field, Tulaiha ran away to Syria after his defeat in the pitched battle that ensued. His confederate tribes became Muslims under the force of circumstances. Khalid did not accept their acceptance of Islam till they returned those who had either killed or burnt the Muslims. They were put to death in a very exemplary manner. Khalid Bin Walid (R.A.A.) informed the Caliph about the victory, acceptance of Islam of the renegades and the retribution of the Muslims who had been killed before. Upon this, the Caliph wrote:

(4)

"May Allah will that these successes become the forerunner of future victories and achievements. God helps those who fear Him and do virtuous deeds.

"Lo! Allah is with those who keep their duty unto Him and those who are doers of good."

(Al-Quran, 16:128)

Exert all your energies for the eradication of the renegades and consequent dominance of Islam. There should be no slackening in the least in this regard. Whoso killed a Muslim, if he falls into your hands, do kill him in such a way as to be a source of lesson for others. Those who transgressed the commandment of Allah, and are the enemies of Islam, they can be put to sword provided this can prove beneficial to the cause of Islam. "

(Saif bin Umar, Tabari, Vol. III, P. 233).

The letter reported in Iktifa, on the authority of Sharik Fazari, is entirely different in letter and spirit from Saif bin Umar's despatch reproduced above. Difference of words can he ignored but the contrast in content and meaning is vital. According to the opinion of Saif-bin-Umar, the Caliph had commissioned Khalid bin Walid (R.A.A.) two important tasks — namely:

(i) to call Tulaiha and his confederates to abandon apostasy movement and fight against them if they do not accept this offer, and

(ii) to take vengeance of those Muslims who were killed mercilessly by the confederates of Tulaiha. After the execution of the above mentioned two missions, Khalid (R.A.A.) was required to wait till further instructions. Saif had narrated another version on the authority of other important personages, according to which Khalid (R.A.A.) was to proceed to Bul'aho to teach a lesson to Malik-bin Nuwaira, a chieftain of Banu Hanzala (a branch of the tribe of Tamim). Malik did not pay Zakat and his fealty to Islam had become dubious. It is evident from the letter of Hadrat Abu Bakr (R.A.A.) reported in Iktifa relating to the Conquest of Bazakha that Khalid-bin-Walid (R.A.A.) was directed to proceed to Yamamah to fight against Musailimah after dealing with Tulaiha. According to Saif the expedition of Yamamah was entrusted to Ikrimah bin Abu Jehl and not to Khalid-binWaleed (R.A.A.).

(5)

"May it be clear that your emissary came here along with your letter, in which you have mentioned regarding the chastizement of Asad and Ghatfan, and the God given victory in Bazakha and further stated that now you are heading towards Yamamah. As I have already advised you, fear Allah, the One without partner, and treat your fellow Muslims with kindness and affection. O'Khalid bin Walid (R.A.A.) Keep away from the haughty of the Banu Mughirah. I have set aside the recommendations of one whose advice I never ignore i.e. Hadrat Umar bin Khattab (R.A.A.). When you reach Banu Hanifa, act with extreme prudence. You have not encountered the enemy of his calibre so far, because his whole tribe is against you from beginning to end and their area is also very vast. When you arrive there, manage the entire affairs by yourselves. Sincere officers should be appointed on Right, Left Wings and other contingents of the army. Consult the distinguished Companions of the Prophet of Allah (S.A W.), be fully considerate to their status and rank. When Banu Hanifa arrange their ranks and files to fight with you, you should also do the same. If they use shafts, you should also do the same. If they attack with spears, you should apply the same; and when they fight with the sword which is fatal, you should also use the sword to fight. If Allah grants you victory over them, beware you would never show any clemency to them, their wounded should be killed; those who run away from the battlefield they should be chased and whoso falls into your hands either he should be put to the sword or burnt in fire. These instructions should not be violated under any circumstances and Peace be upon you."

(Iktifa, P. 252)

(6)

LETTER TO 'IKRIMA BIN ABI JEHL (R.A.A.)

After Tulaiha, Musailimah was the most dangerous enemy, whose drum of prophethood was being trumpeted throughout Yamamah. Ten thousands braves of Banu Hanifa (forty thousand according to Saif) were ready to shed their blood for him. Musailimah had organized his army with great tact and acumen, armed it with huge expenses and was very popular among Bani Hanifa. They used to declare, "Why should we believe in the Prophet of Quraish? We will believe in the messenger of our own (tribe)." Hadrat Abu Bakr Siddiq (R.A.A.) appointed Ikrima bin Abi Jehl for his chastizement. When Ikrimah reached Yamamah, it came to his knowledge that the Caliph (R.A.A.) had sent another army under Shuraihbeel bin Hasana and it will join him soon. 'Ikrima was cut to the quick because he wanted to take the credit of destroying Musailimah without any partner by himself alone. The loyal fierceful fighters of Musailimah created havoc in the rank and file of the Muslim army and 'Ikrima ran away from the battle-field after a crushing defeat. When Hadrat Abu Bakr (R.A.A) came to know of this incident, he was extremely angry upon the conduct of Ikrima and the following furious letter was despatched to him.

"O son of the mother of Ikrima, (after this defeat) neither shall I see your face again nor you will see mine. Do not return here otherwise the morale of the people will be lowered. Go straight to Huzaifah and "Arfajah and fight along with them against the apostates of the Arabs of "Umman and Mahrah If they are already engaged in the battle, you should continue your march and whomso tribe you meet, bring them back to the fold of Islam after proper repentance from apostasy till you and Muhajir bin Abi Umayyah meet each other in Yemen. And Hadaramaut."

(*Saif bin Umar, Tabari*, Vol. III, P. 243).

Saif bin Umar has reported this letter with a little variation in words on the authority of different scholars of history in connection with the Apostasy Movement in Umman, Mahrah, and Yemen.

(See *Tarabi*, P. 262, Vol. III).

(7)

ANOTHER VERSION OF THE LETTER

You are ignorant of the art of teaching others and feel diffident to be taught. The day you meet me, I shall teach you a lesson that you will remember. Why did you not wait till such time as Shuraihbeel joined you and should have fought with his help? Now go to Huzaifa and help him. If he does not need re-inforcement, you may go to Yaman and Hadaramaut and help Muhajir-bin-Ummayyah.

(*Nasikh-ut-Tawqrikh* by Mohammad Taqi, Bombay, Vol. II P. 87).

(8)

TO SHURAIHBEEL-BIN-HASANA (R.A.A.)

Shuraihbeel (R.A.A.) was on his way when he received

the news of the defeat of 'Ikrimah. He stopped where he was, and wrote to the Caliph (R.A.A.) for further instructions under the new situation. Hadrat Abu Bakr Siddiq (R.A.A.) wrote to him to stop where he was for the time being till Khalid-bin-Walid (R.A.A.) was appointed (commissioned) for Yamamah expedition and then wrote to Shuraihbeel:

"When Khalid (R.A.A.) joins you after the successful completion of Yamamah expedition, turn your attention towards the tribe of Quzaah and chastize the rebels of Quzaah who refuse to accept Islam and are bent upon opposing it. This should be executed along with 'Amr bin 'Aas (R.A.A.).

(Saif bin Umar, Tabari, Vol. III, P. 243)

(9)

TO KHALID BIN WALEED (R.A.A.)

In 12 A.H. the famous battle of Yamamah was fought which is not only the greatest battle of the apostasy movement but it may be considered the fiercest fight of the Arabian peninsula. Musailimah's army consisted of ten thousand strong and the Muslim army comprised of six to seven thousand men. According to another version, both the parties had approximately four thousand strong. The fighting force of Musailimah was full of zeal and exemplary devotion. On the contrary, the army of Khalid bin Waleed (R.A.A.) consisted of a great portion of the Arabs who have been mobilized due to reasons of expediency and consideration of sustenance. The Muslims were repulsed thrice during the battle that ensued. The army of Musailimah entered the Muslim camp by force and their defeat was imminent but the Ansar and Muhajirs of Madina pounced upon the enemy fearlessly. Seeing them, the bedouins who were fleeing away from the battlefield also came back. During the battle that ensued there was massacre all round; the Muslims got the upper hand, repulsing the enemy till he sought shelter in the four walls of a garden. Again here a bloody battle was fought in which Musailimah and his many followers were killed. A reporter has presented the picture of the battle field in the following words:

Banu Hanifa inflicted the severest injuries to the Muslims as compared to other enemies. They brought death and destruction for them, and drew upon their poisonous swords even before the use of lancets and arrows. The Muslims faced the enemy with patience and self-control, but the entire battle depended upon seasoned trusted warriors of Islam i.e. the (Muhajirs and Ansar) Abbad bin Bishr Kharashi was inviting to the battlefield like a ferocious tiger calling, "Is there anyone who can encounter me?" One sentimental young Hanafi came before him like a shouting camel and used to say, "Come on, O Khazraji you would be thinking that we are also coward like those with whom you had fought before." Abbad moved towards him but the said Hanafi attacked him before his sword which was broken at that moment and Abbad did not receive any injury, then he attacked him (Hanafi) with his sword and chopped off his feet Hanafi with great difficulty stood up by his knees and called on him saying. "O gentlemen, I request you to put an end to my life." Abbad returned and cut off his neck. Then again, another Hanafi took his place. He and Abba encountered each other. Abbad who was already extremely wounded attacked on his shoulder with such force and velocity that his lung became visible and said, "Take it. This is the turn of the son of Waqsh, I am here." Again he marched forward wounding the Hanfis,

(Iktifa, P. 255, reported by Dhamurah bin Saeed Mazini).

Now we come to the opinion of Khalid bin Waleed about the Hanafis narrated by another reporter:

"I participated in twenty battles, but I did not come across an example of such patience with which the Banu Hanifa endured the attacks of swords, the acumen with which they displayed their skill in the art of use of sword and the steadfastness with which they remained firm in the battle of Yamamah."

(Iktifa, P 257).

More than twelve hundred Muslims were martyred and several thousand wounded. A person who actually participated in the battle reported that a few among the Muhajirs and Ansar joined the congregational prayers with Khalid bin Waleed (R.A.A.) due to the majority being wounded.

(Iktifa, P 252).

Reaching near Yamamah Khalid (R.A.A.) had despatched a forerunner of the army (Scouts) to know the conditions of the people around. There they found a respectable headman of the tribe of Yamamah, Muja'ah bin Mararah was returning to Yamamah along with twenty three men after the execution of an expedition. The Scouts of the army arrested them and brought them to Khalid (R.A.A.). Muja'ah said, "We are neither the enemies of the Muslims nor the spies of Banu Hanifa. We had been to take vengeance of one person from our tribesmen. I accepted Islam by presenting myself before the Messenger of Allah (S.A.W.) and am so." Khalid (R.A.A.) asked the companions of Muja'ah about Musailimah. They said that they believe that he was the messenger of God. Khalid (R.A.A.) ordered them to be killed. Some one recommended that Muja'ah should be kept alive as he is the leader of Banu Hanifa and can be of help in war and peace. Khalid (R.A.A.) ordered Muja'ah to he fettered and soon began to acknowledge the sincerity and sagacity of Muja'ah. So he became the advisor and favourite of Khalid (R.A.A.). Khalid (R.A.A.) was fascinated by the charm of the daughter of Muja'ah, who was renowned for her beauty throughout Yamamah. Khalid (R.A.A.) sent word for her marriage to her father, Muja'ah, who accepted it, but requested him to wait for some time till the wounds of battle are healed up, and grief among the rank and file of the army be subsided as he apprehended that the Caliph (R.A.A.) and the people might feel it. Khalid (R.A.A.) did not wait and the marriage was consummated. Firstly, both the Muhajirs and Ansar, who were mourning the death of their kiths and kins (beloved ones) and whose wounded in thousands were groaning due to the pain of their wounds, did not approve of the marriage and also complained to the Caliph Hadrat Abu Bakr (R.A.A.) felt grieved; Umar bin Khattab (R.A.A.) also threw light on the indulgence and imbalance attitude of Khalid (R.A.A.), so Abu Bakr's (R.A.A.) grief and uneasiness was further aggravated. Even then the Caliph (R.A.A.) did not lose temper. He did not take any action against him but only contented himself with the following warning:

"O, the son of the mother of Khalid! You are very impatient, you enjoy and consummate marriage although the blood of more than twelve hundred Muslims did not dry yet. Then again, Muja'ah had deceived you, and kept you away from the rightful action and used for peace on behalf of his nation (tribe of Banu Hanifa) although God had given you full control over them." *Here the reporter leaves the letter incomplete as it is, and stated that its full contents have been described by Wasmiah in his book.* "The Apostasy or Ar-rid-dah."

(Only the italicised portion is found in *Iktifa, P.* 260 and *Ibn-e-Ishaque, Tabari,* Vol. III, Page 254).

The full story of the peace concluded by Muja'ah and his deception is that after the end of war, Khalid (R.A.A..) along with Muja'ah went out in the battlefield to search for the dead body of Musailimah that was lying somewhere among the many hundred of the dead. When Muja'ah showed the dead body of Musailimah, Khalid (R.A.A.) said, "This is the person who brought havoc upon you. How foolish the Hanafis are! They could be duped by this hated Armenian (as Musailimah was an ugly person of short stature)." Muja'ah said, "No doubt, this is done, but do not be mistaken that the war has ended due to the fact that their leader has been killed. By God! their fresh re-enforcements have arrived to fight against you. Their majority of youngmen and respectable persons are there in the fortress.

(Iktifa, P 259 and *Ibn-e-Ishaque, Tabari, Vol.* III, P. 251).

Although, Khalid (R.A.A.) was puzzled due to this conversation of Muja'ah but at the same time he ordered his army to be ready to fight. The reporter narrates that now the Muslims did not want to fight with Banu Hanifa. They were tired due to war, majority of them has been killed and those survived, majority of them had been wounded. At this time Muja'ah acted with prudence and said to Khalid (R.A.A.), "I am your well-wisher. Both you and Banu Hanifa have been beaten badly. Come on, I sue for settlement of peace on their behalf." The reporter narrates that the old veterans of army of Islam and experienced companions of the Prophet of Allah had been killed and thus the military might of Khalid (R.A.A.) had been reduced considerably and their camels had been emaciated due to scarcity of fodder. Therefore, they wanted that an honourable peace may be effected. This was done, accordingly Banu Hanifa had to surrender their gold, silver, weapons, horses in toto and half the prisoners to the Muslims. After the execution of the said treaty, Khalid (R.A.A.) went along with Muja'ah to inspect the settlement of the Hanafis, saw in their fortresses only women, children and disabled persons, Khalid (R.A.A.) became furious and said to Muja'ah, "You have deceived me. Where are those war veterans and fighting force with which you threatened me?" Muja'ah said, "I was forced to do this for my nation (tribe of Banu Hanifa)." By the conclusion of this peaceful agreement, all Hanafis accepted Islam.

(Iktifa, P. 260).

THE REPLY OF KHALID BIN WALEED (R.A.A.) TO THE LETTER OF CALIPH HADRAT ABU BAKR (R.A.A.)

On receipt of the letter of Hadrat Abu Bakr Siddiq (R.A.A.) on the consummation of marriage with the daughter of Muja'ah, Khalid (R.A.A.) said, "This is all mischief of Hadrat Umar (R.A.A.)." There was some misunderstanding between the two. Khalid (R.A.A.) wrote in self-defence, absolving himself of the censure passed by the first Caliph of Islam, Hadrat Abu Bakr (R.A.A.), mentioning the four objections:

(a) Khalid (R.A.A.) married the daughter of Muja'ah as soon as the war ended.

(b) Commanded the battle-field in a dejective manner and kept himself aloof from the dangers of war.

(c) Did not feel sorry for the many hundred martyrs of his army.

(d) Was led to be deceived by Muja'ah.

Khalid (R.A.A.) replied:

"By my soul! I did not marry with women until and unless I achieved complete victory in the battle and consequent happiness of the same, and shifted from the Camp to the homely atmosphere. I have joined in relationship with such a person that if I had to come from Madinah for this purpose, I would have done so gladly. From the contents and spirit of your letter I presume that I have been charged with a complaint that I did not bemoan properly the death of the martyrs who fell in the battlefield. I can assure you that I have grieved immensely on account of their death. If the sorrow of the living could keep the persons alive or the bemoaning of some one could bring back to life the dead ones, certainly my grief and sorrow should have produced such an effect. Believe me, the zeal of martyrdom took me to such dangerous spots that there was no hope to survive and I was sure of my death. Regarding your assertions that Muja'ah had refrained me from the right course of action, I may, respectfully, submit that I did not then consider my judgment wrong and moreover I had no knowledge of the unknown that could discover the deceit of Muja'ah. No doubt, the peace brought immense advantages to the Muslims by the Grace of God. They have been made the custodians and heirs of the land of Banu Hanifa as well as blessed with the bounties of the virtuous i.e. gold and silver of Banu Hanifa fell into the hands of the Muslims."

The reputed companion of the Prophet of Allah (S.A.W.) Abu Barzah Aslami (R.A.A.) brought this letter to Madina: the wrath of Hadrat Abu Bakr (R.A.A.) slowed down after going through the contents of the above letter. The reporter declares that Hadrat Umar (R.A.A.) remained unmoved and was not affected in the least by this letter, who along with other veterans from the Quraish was as before condemning Khalid (R.A.A.) Abu Barzah (R.A.A.) could not held delivering the following speech in support of Khalid (R.A.A.) which almost pacified the anger of Abu Bakr Siddiq (R.A.A.).

In *Iktifa*, another letter has been stated to have been written by Khalid bin Walid (R.A.A.) in connection with the battle of Yamamah. A few companions of the army of Khalid (R.A.A.) were against the settlement arrived at between him and Muja'ah as the remaining persons from Banu Hanifa were saved from being killed. The Companions (R.A.A.) argued that the settlement is against the guidance of the Caliph of Islam; They further contended that the instructions from the Caliph demand that all the male adult persons of Banu Hanifa should be killed. Khalid (R.A.A.) used to say, "I pay full respect to your arguments but the circumstances are such that action on these instruction is impracticable." The settlement has been executed and complaint of the Companions of the Prophet of Allah (S.A.W.) remained in tact. Khalid bin Walid (R.A.A.)

apprehended that the opposition of the Companions will be almost infectious reaching upto Hadrat Umar Farooq (R.A.A.) and certainly they will instigate the Caliph. Therefore, Khalid (R.A.A.) thought it proper to apprise the Caliph of the Prophet (S.A.W.) of the exceptional circumstances under which he was compelled to agree to sue for peace.

In the name of Allah, All Compassionate and Most Merciful.

TO THE CALIPH OF THE MESSENGER OF ALLAH (S.A.W.) HADRAT ABU BAKR (R.A.A.) FROM KHALID-BIN-WALEED (R.A.A.)

By God, I did not sue for peace with the Hanafi's till the time all those men from my army were killed who were the backbone of my strength. When the horses were reduced like dried thorns and the camels died on account of hunger, so many Muslims were killed and wounded as there was apprehension that either they may be defeated or killed. I used to draw my sword and dashed against the most dangerous points till Allah, the Almighty, blessed us with victory. Thank be to Him."

(Iktifa, 231)

In the actual text there is repetition, expressing restlessness which has been ignored in translation.

(10)

TO KHALID BIN WALEED (R.A.A.)

This despatch was received at a time when peace treaty had been concluded with Muja'ah. The reporter says as if drops of blood were oozing out from this treaty. Several companions (R.A.A.) were opposed to this treaty from the very beginning because they were of the view that this truce was against the very spirit of the intention and guidance (instruction) of the Caliph, Abu Bakr Siddiq (R.A.A.). The readers may recollect that the despatch sent by Caliph Abu Bakr (R.A.A.) on receiving the news of the victory of Buzakha stated, "If God favours you with victory against Banu Hanifa, don't show any leniency to them, their wounded should be put to an end, those who run away, should be chased and whoso falls into your hands should be put to the sword and burnt in the fire." On receiving the above said letter the Companions (R.A.A.) again put pressure on Khalid (R.A.A.) to abrogate the treaty, to surround their forts and after conquering them, all adult males should be put to death. But how Khalid (R.A.A.) could break the treaty which was against the injunctions of the Quran and the Sunnah? He said that the Muslim force had been enfeebled and their horses were so down-trodden to be unable to perform any military service. Had it not been so he would have never executed the treaty.

"On receiving my despatch, act with prudence and if God grants you victory over Banu Hanifa, do not spare alive any male adult amongst them."

(Iktifa, P. 260)

(11)

TO KHALID BIN-WALEED (R.A.A.)

When the emissaries of Khalid (R.A.A.) reached Madina with the news of the conquest of Yamamah, Hadrat Abu Bakr (R.A.A.) enquired about the war and conditions prevailing there. They apprised the Caliph (R.A.A.) that it was the toughest fight that ensued. The army of Musailimah fell upon the Muslims like hungry wolves and repulsed them thrice. The forces of Khalid

(R.A.A.) where the beduin Arabs were in majority could not withstand the enemy and turned their faces from the swords of the enemy. It was the valour and the religious devotion of those Muslims who have seen the Messenger and Prophet of Allah (S.A.W.), kept up the banner of Islam and did not lower it, but they had to pay heavy price for the same. They were killed and wounded in great number. Abu Bakr (R.A.A.) and other Companions (R.A.A.) were highly moved by these details and their hearts were hardened for ever on this account against Banu Hanifa.

"The news that Musailimah was killed in action in the battle has reached here. The conquest of Yamamah and the success of Muslims came also to be known here. The death of Musailimah mean the end of the reputation and strength of the people of Yamamah because an army without its leader is like a body without its head. Now, besiege them in their fortresses and never leave them until and unless subdued completely. Howsoever the people of Yamamah desire to conclude a treaty, you should continue your fight. When the fort is subdued all men (adult male) persons of Banu Hanifa should be killed, their children and women folk should be enslaved, their lands, gold, silver and other properties should be taken possession of."

(*Nasikhut-Tawarikh*, Mohammad Taqi, Bombay).

(12)

TO TURAIFA BIN HAJIZ

Hadrat Abu Bakr (R.A.A.) appointed Turaifa bin Hajiz as Governor (Wali) over those Arabs of Banu Sulaim who had stood firm in Islam. He was a sincere and zealous worker. He delivered speeches so effective that many Arabs of the tribe of Sulaim joined him. The renegades among the Arabs began to loot and plunder. Sometimes Turaifa assaulted them with the help of Muslim companions. This state of affairs—the drama of loot and plunder continued till a person from Banu Sulaim, a dacoit named Iyas came to Hadrat Abu Bakr Siddiq (R.A.A.). As he used to attack the passers by and the habitations, he got the nick name of Fuja'ah. Several expeditions were conducted against the apostates. As a result they were severely punished, so Fuja'ah thought of a mischievous plan by taking into confidence his friend, Najha bin Abi Maisa, who was also a dacoit like him and said, "It is far from me to be a Muslim and I know that I am to die at the hands of the Muslims. Why should I not perform such deeds as may stun the hearts of both, Abu Bakr and Khalid bin Waleed (R.A.A.). He went to Madina and said to the Caliph, "I accepted Islam at the hands of the Messenger of Allah (S.A.W.). I know every nook and corner of the Arabian Peninsula, and also its people as well. Prior to the acceptance of Islam I used to loot and plunder the Arabian tribes. Many tribes of the desert are within my reach, who have turned away from Islam and none of your generals including yourself know them. I can bring them back to the fold of Islam and if they desist I can kill them by their neck. All those renegades from Islam, who are out of the reach of Khalid (R.A.A.), I can catch hold of them, and make fodder of the sword, per chance it may be a source of atonement of my previous sins. But now-a-days my financial condition is weak; neither do I possess money, nor convoys nor weapons of warfare. So kindly help me." Hadrat Abu Bakr (R.A.A.) gave him two horses, thirty camels, weapons for thirty soldiers, and ten Muslims equipped with fodder and weapons

(*Iktifa P. 232*).

Fuja'ah went out towards his tribe and on the way took the Arab apostates With him. When his strength in men increased, he first of all assassinated his Muslim Companions, looted their belongings, ransacked here and there. Sometimes he attacked on one tribe and sometimes on the other. A Muslim party going towards Madina was looted and assassinated by him. On receiving information about the above mentioned incidents, Caliph Abu Bakr (R.A.A.) wrote to his representative in Banu Sulaim, Turaifa:

In the name of Allah, Most Compassionate and Most Merciful

"Peace be upon Turaifa bin Hajiz from the Caliph of the Prophet of Allah (S.A.W.) Abu Bakr (R.A.A.). May it be known to you that Fuja'ah, the enemy of God, came to me and declared himself to be Muslim and requested for necessary paraphernalia for the chastizement of those Arabs who have turned away from Islam. Now I have received authentic news that this enemy of God deprives every body of his belongings whether Muslim or a non Muslim and takes away his weapons and those who do not comply with his orders are killed by his sword. My firm opinion is that you should go along with your Muslim companions for his chastizement. Either kill him or send him to me duly enfettered."

(Tabari, Ibn-Ishaque and *Nasikhut-Twarikh).*

(13)

TO KHALID BIN WALEED (R.A.A.)

When the Caliph of the Messenger of Allah (S.A.W.) Hadrat Abu Bakr (R.A.A.) came to know the heresy and corruption on earth spread by Fuja'ah! he wrote the following to Khalid bin Waleed :

"If you attain victory over Banu Hanifa by the Grace of God, do not stay for long, in Yamamah, go over to the tribal area of Banu Sulaim and inflict upon them such an exemplary punishment that they remember for ever. I do not feel more angry against any other tribe that Banu Sulaim. Their Chief Fuja'ah, came to me and said, "I am a Muslim, help me for Jehad. I gave him camels and weapons. Then he embarked upon plunder and loot. If you overpower them by the Grace of God, I shall be least angry with you if you burn them in fire and kill them without any hesitation, so that they may learn a lesson of indulging in rebellion and treachery in future."

On receipt of the above letter Khalid (R.A.A.) despatched the Sappers and Miners of the army. Banu Sulaim among whom the majority formed part of Banu-Us-saiya were the most turbulent, and they became ready for war against the Muslims. Abu Shajara son of the famous poet Khansa, was their head and leader. They assembled near the pond, named Juwa', situated in the vicinity of pasture in the north-east of Madina. Khalid (R.A.A.) encamped his army in front of them. The Muslims were less in number, the after effects of the battle of Yamamah were still there, the wounds of the injured were not yet healed up, the condition of the cavalry was very unsatisfactory due to the scarcity of food and fodder. During the battle that ensued, the Muslims were outnumbered by Banu Sulaim. Khalid (R.A.A.) himself plunged into the battlefield, so fought and commanded the army that the enemy gave way and their soldiers were caught by the Muslims.

(*Iktifa*. P. 264)

(14)

TO 'AMR BIN AL-'AAS (R.A.A) AND WALEED BIN 'UQBAH

Hadrat Abu Bakr (R.A.A.) appointed 'Amr bin Al-'Aas (R.A.A.) and Walid bin Uqbah (R.A.A.) as Collectors of Zakat in different Arab Settlements. When they reached their respective destinations to take charge of their offices, they received the following directive from the Caliph of Islam (R.A.A.)

"Fear God in every matter, open or secret. Whoso fears God, He resolves their difficulties and gives them benefit from a place one cannot imagine. The person who fears Allah, considering His Omnipresence, God forgives his omissions and commissions and rewards him handsomely. No doubt, the best and the most beneficial mission for human beings is to preach and persuade each other, to entertain fear of God, You are on the Godly way entrusted to you, do not be negligent or delay the performance of duty entrusted to you. Do not show negligence in any matter relating to the existence of your *Deen* (Islam) or the maintenance of your prestige. You are again advised finally to be dutiful efficient and not easy-going."

(Kanzul-'Ummal Qasim bin Muhammad).

REBELLION IN YAMAN

The brief, pithy and comprehensive as well, despatch addressed to the Himyari chiefs of Yaman is to be understood in its historical perspective and the then existing political set up. Nearly forty seven years before the Hijra of the Prophet of Allah (S.A.W.) to Madina, Iran (then known as Persia) had occupied Yaman. The Messenger of Allah (S.A.W.) had sent an invitation to accept Islam to the ruler of Yaman, who readily accepted the same and the Prophet of Islam (S.A.W.) kept restored him kingdom. In 9 A.H. he died and in 10 A.H. the Prophet of Allah (S.A.W.) appointed Collectors of Zakat and divided Yaman into seven provinces for the purpose. Mu'az bin Jabal (R.A.A.) was the eighth one who was overall governor of the area. In addition to this he was also responsible to teach the people in the jurisprudence of Islam and the Quran. At this time Yaman had a very clever man in the person of Aswad 'Ansi whose lineage reached the ancient ancestor of the country namely Saba. He proclaimed himself to be the Prophet with a burning desire to rule the country. During the days of Ibn Bazam, his grip was very strong in the country; but after his death, Yaman was divided into seven parts due to administrative reasons and Aswad got a suitable opportunity to fulfil his ambition. The people of his tribe had already rallied round him. The original inhabitants of Yaman, relating to Saba and Hamurabi Himyar tribes and the other respectable strata of society were from Persia of the Aba race known as Abnaa, who were respectable people in the Yaman Society, and held important official posts in the State from the days of Kaiser. Their important leaders, Shahr bin Bazaam, Feroze Dailami and Zazawia had already accepted Islam. They fought their counterpart Aswad but in the end they could not withstand against Aswadi chiefs and their chief leader, Shahr bin Bazaam, ruler of San'aa, had been assassinated, and other leaders also fled to different parts of the country including Madina. As soon as the Prophet of Allah (S.A.W.) was apprised of the deteriorating situation in Yaman, the Messenger of Islam (S.A.W.) sent despatches to Aswad and other Yamani leaders. Aswad 'Ansi remained unmoved but other chiefs in Yaman like Amir bin Shehr, Saeed bin Aqib etc. obeyed the orders of the Prophet (S.A.W.), and were ready to help the Muslims. Intoxicated by the pelf and power of Yaman, Aswad 'Ansi became proud and haughty. Consequently he showed indignation to the Commander-in-Chief of his army, Qais-bin-Abd Yaghus (Makshooh Muradi) and other leaders from the Abnaa Section of the Yaman Population, Feroze and Zazawia — who needed help and succour against Aswad which came from the Prophet of Allah (S.A.W.). The prestige and power of Aswad 'Ansi could not last long. For more than four months and he was assassinated in his own palace. Soon after the assassination of Aswad, the Prophet of Islam (S.A.W.) also passed away from this world, whose work was continued by his Caliph, Hadrat Abu Bakr (R.A.A.). Yaghus was a powerful and influential commander. Able, full of determination, he was always on the look out to eradicate the Persian portion of the Yaman population, namely Abnaa. He further conspired with the Aswadi military leaders to turn out the Abnaa from the country but on this account he was not on good terms with other important leaders —Feroze, and Zazawia, who was assassinated by means of deception and Feroze had his hair-breadth, escape who wrote to the Caliph for help, apprising him of the entire political situation then prevailing in Yaman. In the above mentioned historical perspective, Hadrat Abu Bakr (R.A.A.) examined the situation in circumspection and the following letter was despatched to the various chiefs in Yaman:

(15)

TO YAMANI CHIEFS

"From Abu Bakr (R.A.A.), the Caliph of the Messenger of Allah (S.A.W.) to Umair bin Aflah zi Maran, Saeed bin Aqib Zizood, Sumaifa bin Nakoor zi Kala', Hushab zi Zulaim and Shehr zi Naiyaf.

Those who are bent upon harming the Abnaa' and wish to fight against them, you should help the Abnaa against them, Take Abnaa under your escort, obey Feroze and act according to his advice. Fight against the rebels. I have appointed Feroze the Commander-in-Chief of the forces. Help him against the enemy.

(Saff bin Umar, Tabari, Vol. III, P. 218-266).

(16)

TO TAHIR BIN ABI HALA

The despatches sent to different chiefs of different tribes of Arabia by Hadrat Abu Bakr (R.A.A.) are political cum historical in nature. They deal with the then existing conditions of Arabia, similarly the despatch sent to Tahir bin Abi Hala, he speaks of the same situation. In order to appreciate its full significance it is necessary to understand the historical cum-political perspective of the time. In the West of Yaman and South of Red Sea, there is a strip of land known Tihama, containing many low-lying rocks stretching upto San'aa, the capital of Yaman, and Mecca on the other side. Tihama was a district of Yaman, containing several villages and towns which became one of the seven provinces on the demise of Ibn Bazam, the ruler of Yaman. In 10 A.H., the Prophet of Allah (S.A.W.) appointed Tahir bin Ahi Hala as governor of Tihama, inhabited by two strong and vital tribes — Ghak and Ash'ar. There was also a commercial highway leading to Aden from Mecca along Red Sea. The dacoits from Ghak and Ash'ar were the first to raise the standard of rebellion against Islam as soon as news reached them of the demise of the Prophet of Allah (S.A.W.). They started loot and plunder on this commercial high way and seceded from the local governor, Tahir bin Abi Hala. Many disgruntled elements rallied round them for the time being. They were ill-equipped, ill-fed and almost without a leader. During the battle that ensued they were killed in large number. The highway was almost pitted with corpses, the news of victory had not reached Madina so far but the following letter of Hadrat Abu Bakr (R.A.A.) was received by Governor Tahir bin Abi Hala in reply to his letter No. 17.

"Received your letter in which you have intimated the news of your military expedition regarding chastizement of the goondas in 'Alaab with the help of the people of the Chief of Ak, Masrooq. You have taken right step in the right direction. Do not hesitate in punishing them without showing leniency. Stay on in 'Alaab till the highway is cleared of the danger of the goondas and receive further instructions from the Centre."
(Tabari, Vol. III, P. 200).

(17)

TO 'AT-TAAB BIN USAID (R.A.A.)

Caliph of the Messenger of Allah (S.A.W.), Abu Bakr Siddiq (R.A.A.), sent a general order to all the governors to punish the rebels with the aid of the faithful Arabs and the governors of Mecca and Najran were further instructed to wait for his further orders to proceed further for battle after repulsing the rebels. The firm intention of Hadrat Abu Bakr (R.A.A.) was to merge the loyal militia of the area with the forces under Usama bin Zaid, quell the rebellion in Yaman after his return from syria. Among the officers of the mid area of Mecca and Najran, one was Usman bin Abil-as Saqfi, governor of Taif, who was commissioned to raise an army to keep ready and the other one, was 'At-Taab bin Usaid to whom following despatch was sent:

"From the Emirate of Mecca raise a militia of five hundred youths and entrust their command to a person in whom you confide."

(*Tarikh-ul-Maluk war-rusul, Tabari*, Vol. III P. 266).

(18)

ADDRESSED TO MUHAJIR BIN UMAYYA

The above despatch sent by Hadrat Abu Bakr (R.A.A.) needs to be reviewed under circumspection. As already stated Qais bin Makshooh was under the intoxication of tribal jealousy in Yaman, who wanted to extirpate the Persian Abnaa from Yaman and exercise full control over the country. Zazawia was assassinated, Feroze had his hair-breadth escape in a Yamani tribe, whose head was his close relation. The Yamani chiefs could not be of much help because their men had joined Qais, so Feroze had to raise his own militia based upon his own resources. In the first instance, he freed the Abnaa, who were being expelled by the land route and thereafter met Qais near San'aa. During the battle that ensued Qais was defeated. In this connection it will be not out of place to mention that Caliph Abu Bakr (R.A.A.) wrote urgent letters to Tahir bin Abi Hala, Governor of Tihama, the eastern portion of Yaman and the chief of the tribe of

'Akk, Masrooq. The third despatch was sent to a very faithful chief of Tihana to raise an army and wait military action till receipt of the instructions of the Caliph of Prophet of Allah (S.A.W.). Soon thereafter, Hadrat Abu Bakr (R.A.A.) despatched reinforcements in men, and weapons under the command of Muhajir bin Ummayyah, who had been the governor of the place during the days of the Prophet of Allah (S.A.W.). He was commanded to quell the rebellion and help Feroze. Muhajir reached Najran along with the chief of Tihama, duly reinforced with an army raised from the tribesmen met on the way. Observing the situation mentioned above, Qais and his allies were demoralised, majority of his men fled from the battlefield and he surrendered unconditionally. Muhajir arrested Qais. When the Caliph Abu Bakr (R.A.A.) came to know this, he wrote to Mujahir:

"Send Qais bin Makshooh to me duly enchained."

When this daring rebel reached Madina, Hadrat Umar Farooq (R.A.A.) advised Caliph Abu Bakr (R.A.A.) to kill him as he had assassiisnated Zazawia and embarked upon a career of loot and plunder. Qais swore that he did not kill Zazawia. In fact, Caliph Abu Bakr (R.A.A.) wished to forgive him to get benefit out of his experience and bravery Seeing the insistence of Umar Farooq Hadrat Abu Bakr (R.A.A.) said to Qais "If you swear fifty times near the pulpit of the Prophet of Allah (S.A.W.) that you have not killed Zazawia then I can forgive you." Qais swore and thus saved himself. During the wars that ensued later on, he rendered valuable services to the cause of Islam as envisaged by the Caliph of the Messenger of Allah (S.A.W.) (*Saif bin Umar Tabari and Kanzul 'Ummal*).

(19)

DOCUMENT GIVEN TO THE CHRISTIANS OF NAJRAN

In 10 A.H. the Christians of Najran refused to accept Islam, the Prophet of Allah (S.A.W.) had given them security of life, property and religion in lieu of payment of a fixed annual subsidy under a documentary covenant wherein the above stated conditions were written. After the demise of the Prophet of Islam (S.A.W.), military action started against the rebels, the Christians of Najran also apprehended danger lest they may be chastized, so they sent a deputation to the Caliph of the Prophet of Allah (S.A.W.), Abu Bakr (R.A.A.) had desired the reaffirmation of the covenant reached during the days of the Messenger of Allah (S.A.W.). The Caliph acceded to their desire and executed the following document.

This is a covenant from the Caliph of Muhammad, the Messenger of Allah (S.A.W.). Abu Bakr (R.A.A.) to the Christians of Najran.

Full protection is accorded from Allah and His Prophet (S.A.W.) to the Christian inhabitants of Najran regarding their life, land, nationhood, property and wealth, even to those who are residing as their dependants in the vicinity and villages of Najran and to those living in Najran and outside the country, their priests, monks, churches, and everything whether great and small. They will neither be subjected to military service nor will be treated harshly, nor their priests will be forced to relinquish their asceticism. This covenant is the reaffirmation and ratification of the original document executed by the Prophet of Allah (S.A.W.) with the people of Najran. Whatever is contained in the above document, Allah and His Messenger (S.A.W) stand witness to it. It is incumbent upon the Christian inhabitants of Najran to fulfil their responsibilities with sincerity and truth."

(*Kitabul-Kharaj, Abu Yusuf*).

REBELLION IN BAHRAIN

(20)

TO 'ALA BIN HADHRAMI (R.A.A.)

In the days of Hadrat Abu Bakr's Caliphate, Bahrain— the strip of land then known running from the Delta of Iraq upto the present state, Qatr, was under the domain of ruler of Hira, were dependent upon the Persian Emperors, Kisras. The land then known as Bahrain comprised of the famous cities — Hajar, Khatt, Juwasa Qatif, Arab, Banunah, Zara, Saboor, Darin, (Jazira) Ghaba and Mushaqqar. On the coastal cities of commercial activity in Bahrain there was mixed population — the Persians, Christian, Jews, Jatt and the Arabs. In commerce the Persians had the upper hand. Behind the coastal cities of Bahrain there were three important tribes with their manifold branches, Bikr bin Wail, Abdul Qais, and Rabia. A large number of their families were Christians whose main occupation was to rear horses, camels, sheep, and lastly to implant date-trees. The head of these tribesmen were those who could gain confidence of the Hira government. One of them was Alunzar bin Sawee, an inhabitant of Hajar, ruling the tribesmen of his vicinity, Abdul Qais. In 8 A.H. the Prophet of Allah (S.A.W.) sent Ala bin Hadhrami to invite Munzar and governor of Hajar to accept Islam. Munzar and his tribe, Qais, became Muslims. The Persians, Christians and the Jews of Hajar accepted to pay Jaziya with great reluctance. The rest of the habitations of Bahrain did not accept Islam. In 11 A.H. soon after the demise of the Prophet of Allah (S.A.W.), Munzar also passed away. Their departure from this world was a great signal for rebellion throughout. Jardu, the leader of Abu Qais had been in the company of the Prophet of Allah (S.A.W.), so he remained firm Muslim and his tribesmen also covenanted to stick to Islam. This was due to his exertations. The rest of the

Arabs and the non-Arabs decided to shake off the yoke of allegiance from Madina. The Iranian Government encouraged the rebels and gave the command of the rebels to an Arab commander. The representative of the Messenger of Allah (S.A.W.), Aban bin Saeed bin 'Aas returned to Madina after observing the clouds of rebellion in Hajar. Abu Bakr Siddiq (R.A.A.) sent a small contingent of force to Hajar under 'Ala bin Hadhrami, who joined hands with the faithful tribesmen of Abdul Qais. The leader of the rebels Hutam Sa'labi, came with an army; during the battle that ensued the Muslims were repulsed and took shelter in a fortress, Juwasa and waited for reinforcements. The belligerents were highly intoxicated during the night and 'Ala, taking advantage of the situation, attacked them with full might. The soldiers of the enemy were killed in large numbers, many of them took to flight and the rest of them were done away with by 'Ala, who regained Hajar. But his position was still far from being secure as the local Persians were spreading rumours that Mafrooq, the leader of Shaibani, was on his way with an army to over throw the Madina Govt. The moment Caliph Abu Bakr (R.A.A.) came to know of it, he sent the following despatch to 'Ala bin Hadhrami:

"If it is established after investigation that Shaiban Bin S'aliba, whose leader is Mafrooq are to attack you, send an army to rout Banu Shaiba and terrorize their hinder tribesmen to the extent that they may never pluck courage to raise heads against you."

(*Tabari, Vol. III, P. 261*).

(21)

ADDRESSED TO ANAS BIN MALIK (R.A.A.)

The clouds of rebellion were hovering over the Islamic World when Abu Bakr (R.A.A.) took over as Caliph of the Prophet of Allah (S.A.W.). The imperative need of the hour was men and money. Islam was a dominant force in Bahrain at that time, the local inhabitants— Persians, Christians and the Jews used to pay Jiziya and the Arab Muslims, whose main occupation was to rear camels and sheep, paid Zakat. In order to consolidate the Kharaj income from Bahrain, Hadrat Abu Bakr (R.A.A.) appointed Anas bin Malik (R.A.A.) as their collector of Zakat. He was energetic young man of hardly 20 or 21 years, full of zeal, whose main characteristic was that he knew the art of reading and writing and had been in the company of the Prophet of Allah (S.A.W.) for more than ten years. He was entrusted with the following schedule of Collection of Zakat by Hadrat Abu Bakr (R.A.A.).

"The schedule of Zakat is reproduced below which was enjoined by Allah and the Holy Prophet of Allah (S.A.W.) levied the same upon the Muslims, who were directed to pay according to fixed rate and not more than those fixed for the purpose:

On every five camels upto twenty four, one sheep is payable as Zakat;
from twenty five to thirty five Camels one *bint-i-Makhaz* (she—camel in the second year of her age) is payable, if the same is not available with the payer, one *ibn-i-laboon* (male camel in his 3 years age) can be paid, from thirty six to forty five — one *bint-laboon* (she-camel in her third year) is to be paid;
from 46 to 60 one *hiqqah* (she — camel in her fourth year):
from 61 to 75, one *jaz'ah'* (she camel in her fifth year);
from 76 to 90-two *bint-i-laboon;* (she camels of 3 years);
from 91 to 120 two *hiqqah* (she camel of 4 years);
After and upward — one *bint-i-laboon* on every 40 camels, and one *hiqqah* on every fifty camels.
There is no Zakat upto four camels, zakat is to be realized

as one she goat when the least number is five.
Whoso is to pay one *jaz'ah* and has none as such, he is allowed to pay one *hiqqah* along with two she-goats or With 20 dirhams.
Whoso is to pay one *hiqqah* but has none, is allowed to pay one *bint-i-laboon* along with two sheeps or with 20 dirhams.
If a person is to pay one *bin-i-laboon* but has hiqqah, he may pay it as zakat but may take two sheep or 20 dirhams from the collector of Zakat to make account equitable,

One she-goat will be realised upto forty sheep,
from 121 to 200, two she-goats are payable;
from 201 to 300 three sheeps as zakat,
from 300 and upwards one sheep will be realized as zakat on every 100 sheep.
Infirm or defective animal should not be paid as zakat and the collector of zakat should not insist for the male (animal) necessary breeding to for the prayer except by the free will of the payer of zakat.
Zakat shall not be realised on less than forty sheep except the one who pays voluntarily.

Zakat at 2½% is to be paid on two hundred dirhams or five ounces (Uqiya) of silver. It is not incumbent to pay on less quantity than the above stated unless one pays by his own free-will.

(Sunan-e-Kubra and Bukhari etc.).

REBELLION IN AMMAN

(22)

TO 'AMR BIN AL-'AAS (R.A.A.)

This is a unique despatch of the Caliph of the Messenger of Allah (S.A.W.), Hadrat Abu Bakr (R.A.A.) addressed to 'Amr bin 'Aas (R.A.A.) in the matter of its reference and context, reproduced by Ibn-e-Asákar in the History of Syria. The letter is reproduced in the words of 'Amr bin al-'Aas (R.A.A.) himself.

"I was appointed Governor of 'Amman by the Prophet of Allah (S.A.W.). When I reached there, the local priests and monks came to me and asked, 'Who are you?' I said, 'My name is 'Amr bin 'Aas. I belong to the tribe of Quraish.' The Priests asked, 'who has sent you? I replied, 'The Messenger of Allah (S.A.W.). The priests further asked, 'Who is the Messenger of Allah (S.A.W.). I replied "Muhammad (S.A.W.) bin Abdullah bin Abdul Mattalib. He is a distinguished personality of our tribe. We know about his genealogy, who has commanded us to be virtuous, avoid evil deeds and worship only One God.' The Priests appointed their representative to hold conversation with me, who asked, 'Is their any sign for his Prophethood (S.A.W.). I said 'Yes, in between his (S.A.W.) two shoulders there is a piece of flesh called seal of Prophethood.' The representative asked, "Does he accept charity.' I said, 'No'. The representative, said, 'What about the gift?' I said, 'Yes, he (S.A.W.) accepts the gift.' The representative: 'When there is fight between him and his nation, who wins?' I said, 'Sometimes they and sometimes we win.' After this conversation the people of Amman became Muslim. Thereafter the representative said, 'By God, if you are truthful as to whatever you have said just now, the Prophet (S.A.W.) passes away from this world to night.'

A few days had passed one camel driver got his camel sit down and asked about 'Amr bin 'Aas. I became perplexed and went to him who gave a letter to me, entitled "From Abu Bakr (R.A.A.), the Caliph of the Messenger of Allah (S.A.W.) to 'Amr bin 'Aas.' I went to the room with the letter, broke open its seal, whose contents were as follows:

In the name of Allah, All Compassionate and Most Merciful

Peace of Allah (Salam) be upon 'Amr bin 'Aas from Abu Bakr (R.A.A.) the Caliph of the Messenger of Allah (S.A.W.). Be it known that whenever Allah, the Almighty, willed, sent the Prophet (S.A.W.), kept him (S.A.W.) alive till the time He willed, and took him (S.A.W.) away from this world according to His Will, Who has said in the Quran:

"Lo! thou will die and lo! they will die."

(39:30)

The Muslims of Madina entrusted the responsibility of leadership of the Ummah (nation) to me, quite contrary to my wishes. I beseach the help and guidance of Allah. When you receive my letter, do not open the rope (of camel) the Prophet of Allah (S.A.W.) had tied down and do not tie the same that had been opened by him (S.A.W.) and Adieu"! (meaning thereby realize zakat of camels according to the injunctions of the Prophet of Allah (S.A.W.).

(*Tarikh-i-Damishq* etc.).

(23)

TO 'IKRIMA BIN ABU JEHL

This despatch is taken from the Conquests of 'Asim Kufi and the later historians have quoted it, for example, the compiler of Nasikhut-Tawarikh: The political perspective is like this:

After the receipt of letter from Hadrat Abu Bakr (R.A.A.), 'Ikrima bin Abu Jehl started for Hadharamaut with two thousand horsemen to help Ziyad bin Lubaid (R.A.A.) On the way the Muslims recruited youngmen from the villages, entered the frontiers of Yaman and reached its capital San'aa, where Aswad 'Ansi's few months rule had toppled down and the flag of Islam was again hoisted. Quite a good number among them had joined the Muslim army, who in the ancient city of Maarib were resting. Recruitment was in progress. On receipt of the information the chiefs of the capital of Daba took it ill that the army under 'Ikrimah is coming to chastize Banu Kinda in support of Ziyad (R.A.A.). They said, "We entertain 'Ikrimah in such a way that he will forget Banu Kinda." So they revolted and Huzaifa bin Yamaan Azdi, then stationed as Collector of Zakat in Oman, hid himself in an unknown secure place in the country, and informed the centre in Madina about the rebellion in Daba. Hadrat Abu Bakr Siddiq (R.A.A.) sent the following order to 'Ikrimah (R.A.A.):

"Let it be known and clear to you that the people of Daba had revolted, so before proceeding towards Ziyad (R.A.A.), you are directed to see that they are thoroughly punished without the least hesitation. When you are victorious over them, send the rebels of Daba to me duly enchained, and proceed further to help Ziyad (R.A.A.), who will be commander of the entire army, punish the unruly with his consultation, and do your utmost with courage. I earnestly hope and fervently pray to Allah that you will be triumphant over Hadhramaut and the fire of rebellion will be soon extinguished."

(Futah, 'Asim Kufi').

According to historical sources available, Hadrat Huzaifa was staying in Tabala, a settlement nearly 200 miles from Mecca. As soon as he received the letter of the Caliph about the rebellion in Daba, he undertook this expedition with two thousand strong, the first armed intervention by Hadrat Abu Bakr (R.A.A.) against the apostates.

REBELLION IN HADRAMAUT AND KINDA

(24)

ADDRESSED TO ZIYAD BIN LUBAID ANSARI (R.A.A.)

This despatch is an extract from '*Iktifa*' and need a little elucidation in its historical perspective. In fact, a deputation from Banu Kinda came to the Prophet of Allah (S.A.W.) in 10 A.H. and gave news that tribe of Banu Kinda had accepted Islam. The Messenger of Allah (S.A.W.) appointed Ziyad bin Lubaid Ansari as governor and Collector of Zakat. During the life time of the Prophet of Allah (S.A.W.) Ziyad realized Zakat from the settlements of Banu Kinda. He was a hard task master Hadrat Abu Bakr (R.A.A.) sent the following despatch with Abu Hind Maula Bani Biyaza:

In the name of Allah, Most Compassionate and Most Merciful

Salam (Peace and blessings of Allah) be upon Ziyad bin Lubaid (R.A.A.) from Abu Bakr (R.A.A.), Caliph of the Messenger of Allah (S.A.W.) I am grateful to One, Whose partner is none in worship. Be it known to you that the Prophet of Allah (S.A.W.) has passed away from this mundane world.

'Lo! we are Allah's and lo! unto Him we are returning?
(Al-Quran 2:156)

With the knowledge that leadership in every action is dependent upon the guidance and help of Almighty Allah, you are hereby directed to pick up the girdle of the loin of your courage and perform such deeds that are befitting to your personality: those who are under your jurisdiction, take the oath of fealty on my behalf from them; whoso refuses to do so, bring him round with the application of sword against him and face the disobedient with the help of the obedient. There is not the least doubt that Allah will dominate His Deen (religion) over all others, howsoever the disbelievers may desist it.

'He may make it (deen) conqueror of all religion, however, much idolaters may be averse."

(*Iktifa*, P. 269).

(25)

ADDRESSED TO ASH'AS BIN QAIS AND OTHER CHIEFS OF BANU KINDA

A continuous account of the rebellion of Banu Kinda in Hadhramaut is to be found in the Conquests of 'Asim Kufi and Nasikhut-Tawarikh by Muhammad Taqi. Ash'as, the most influential leader hailing from the rulers of the kings among the Kindis, was predominant in Hadhramaut at that time and his hold was most effective. The western part of Hadhramaut is a continuous chain of hillocks and dales, consisting many towns and villages with abundance of dates, fodder and a good cultivation of sugar cane and other corns. Quite a good number of forts and fortresses were built on top hills and safely guarded valleys. As has been stated earlier Ash'as and his tribesmen, Kindi, had accepted Islam at the invitation of the Prophet of Islam (S.A.W.), who had appointed Ziyad bin Lubaid Ansari as his representative and Collector of Zakat. He was a very strict officer as reported by a number of chroniclers. After the receipt of letter of Hadrat Abu Bakr (R.A.A.), intimating the demise of the Prophet of Allah (S.A.W.) and consequent oath of fealty. Ash'as and his tribesmen hesitant to take the oath of allegiance were bred in a different atmosphere. They thought that the

Prophet of Allah (S.A.W.) is no more, let a near one among his kith and kins should come forward whom they may accept as their leader, and not the one from Murra tribe Abu Bakr (R.A.A.) who had no social or political distinction. Ash'as and his tribesmen believed in the hereditary monarchy and as such were thinking that a man from the family of the Holy Prophet (S.A.W.) should be appointed as his successor. Contrary to this, his nephew, Imra-ul-Qais bin Abbas, who himself was quite influential among the Kindis, tried to convince Ash'as to accept the verdict of the people of Madina and swore allegiance in favour of the Caliph of the Prophet, Abu Bakr (R.A.A.); but he remained adament and thus the Kindis were torn asunder into tow. Again, the situation was further aggravated on the matter of payment of Zakat between Ziyad (R.A.A.) and other tribesmen of Kindi. The exchange of fiery words in verse compelled Ziyad (R.A.A.) to leave for Madina, but soon on the way, he took courage and tried to convince the Kindis in favour of the new Caliph of the Prophet of Islam (S.A.W.). But he failed and continued his journey and apprised of the entire political situation to the Caliph of the Prophet of Allah (S.A.W.), Hadrat Abu Bakr (R.A.A.). Abu Bakr (R.A.A.) was highly grieved after knowing the conditions prevailing in Hadhramaut. He gave four thousand strong army to Ziyad (R.A.A.) for the chastizement of Bani Kinda, who were struck with terror when they came to know of it. The locality of Ash'as became the hot-bed of discussion, the prudent and the elite advised their men to abandon opposition and advocated peace and obedience while the unruly and the turbulent were bent upon mischief. Ash'as was inclined to obedience to the Caliph (R.A.A.); Ziyad (R.A.A.) displayed extraordinary zeal of the chastizement of those Kindis who were hesitant to take the Oath of Allegiance or refused to do so. He fought against them, their women folk, and children were enslaved and took away their property as booty. Ash'as was already grieved for the loss of so many tribesmen, now his turn came and he had to bear the brunt of the whole situation, who rallied round him with all the available men and material to face Ziyad (R.A.A.) in the city of Taryam in Hadhramaut. Ash'as showed bravery and sincerity in his cause and led his army in such a way that the Muslim army under Ziyad (R.A.A.) gave way and all the routes were blocked so thoroughly that his army was completely cut off, their supplies of food and fodder were stopped. With great difficulty Ziyad (R.A.A.) could inform the Caliphate of the exact situation prevailing there them. Realizing the gravity of the situation and in order to win over Ash'as and other Kindis, Hadrat Abu Bakr (R.A.A.) sent the following despatch in the critical hour.

"I advise you to be steadfast in Islam, do not be led away from the right path; if it is due to the stiff policy of Ziyad (R.A.A.), I dismiss him and appoint an amil (officer) who will treat you well. I have instructed my envoy accordingly. If he finds you readily obedient and repentant not to repeat such activities, he may send Ziyad (R.A.A.) back to me.

(*Futuh, 'Asim* P. 13)

(26)

TO 'IKRIMA BIN ABI JEHL

After reading the above mentioned letter, Ash'as said to the Envoy of the Caliph:

"If we hesitate a little in accepting the Son of Abu Qahafa as Caliph (Abu Bakr Siddiq (R.A.A.) we were dubbed as kafirs (unbelievers) and Ziyad bin Lubaid (R.A.A.) was ordered to kill by the neck the Kindi Chiefs namely my own nephews who were not considered good Muslims (i.e. Kafirs)."

The envoy, whose name is given in *Nasikhut-tawarikh* as Muslim bin Abdullah, refuted the arguments advanced by Ash'as and said:

'When the Ansar and Muhajirs had acknowledged Abu Bakr (R.A.A.) as Caliph of the Prophet (S.A.W.) unanimously and your nephews did not accept him as such, certainly they became Kafirs (unbelievers)."

The envoy could not finish his speech, a passionate youth from the tribe of Banu Kindi and one of the nephews of Ashias became furious and killed the envoy of the Caliph then and there. Ash'as patted him and said that he had done a good deed. This action of the irresponsible youth was highly disapproved by the elders of the Kindi tribesmen, because the letter by the Caliph (R.A.A.) had opened the door of negotiations which they liked from the bottom of the heart. The murder of the envoy again closed the door of peace talks, and consequently several of the Kindi chiefs were highly annoyed on account of the wrongful action and consequent conduct of the Kindi chief namely Ash'as and went away to their respective tribes. The Kindi chief, Ash'as had only two thousand men of his own class, as such his position weakened. Taking advantage of the weak position of his opponent, Muhajir bin Ummayah came out of the fortress of Taryam and gave battle to the enemy on the bank of the river Raqan. Ash'as fought with great sagacity and acumen and gave an almost fatal blow on the head of Muhajir bin Ummayah, who fled away from the battlefield. During the battle that ensued the Muslim forces ran away and many of them were killed in chase by the men of Ash'as, and the rest took shelter in the fort. Ziyad bin Lubaid (R.A.A.) informed the Caliph of his defeat and consequent hide in the Taryam fortress. The Caliph of Islam despatched the following letter to 'Ikrimah:

"Be it known that the standard of rebellion has again been raised by the tribesmen of Kindah and encircled Ziyad bin Lubaid (R.A.A.) and Muhajir bin Ummayyah (R.A.A.). On receipt of this letter, advance towards Taryam at once to chastise the rebels in a befitting manner, recruiting men from the respective tribes on the way including the citizens of Mecca, who may accompany you."

(*Nasikhut-Tawarikh*).

In order to appreciate the exact nature of the campaigns conducted by Ikrimah, it may be recalled that he was one of the eleven Commanders of the army of Islam sent to chastize the apostates during the reign of Abu Bakr (R.A.A.). On receipt of the emergent command of the Caliph of Islam, Abu Bakr (R.A.A.), Ikrimah hastened to proceed to Bukhair Fortress and cut off the third route, stopping supplies to Ash'as thereby weakening his position that led to his surrender. The Caliph had ordered not to kill Ash'as and his men but unfortunately the message reached late and Bukhair was conquered four days earlier and Ziyad bin Lubaid (R.A.A.) invited Ikrimah to share the booty, resulting in a complaint to the Centre and the Caliph ordered:

"Only that person is entitled to share booty who actually participated in the battle."

(*Kanzul 'Ummal*).

Subsequently, Hadrat Umar Farouq (R.A.A.), the Second Caliph of Islam, stated to have ordered:

"Whatever succour (military force) reaches you before the deformation of the dead, killed in action is to share the booty."

(Qazi Abu Yusuf).

(27)

TO MUHAJIR BIN ABI UMAYYAH (R.A.A.)

Muhajir bin Abi Umayyah (R.A.A.) was one of the right lieutenants of Hadrat Abu Bakr (R.A.A.) who was commanded to put an end to nefarious activities of the apostates in Hadharamaut. Ash'as, the main protagonist of the movement, was struck with terror on account of the reinforcements of Muhajir bin Ummayyah (R.A.A.). He took shelter in the hilly fortress of Bukhair, but had to come out of it to face the Muslims due to heavy casualties inflicted upon their own tribesmen, Kindis. Overwhelmed by the forces of Islam, the general massacre of the armed men of Ash'as, extreme scarcity of food, led him to sue for peace which was not acceded to; later on he requested for shelter protection for the nine chiefs of the tribe along with their family members, who were to be sent to the Caliph (R.A.A.) at Madina, for punishment according to the discretion of the Caliph (R.A.A.). This was accepted. The youngmen of the fortress were killed and the Caliph's agent Mughira bin Shu'ba came with the following letter:

"If you receive this letter after you have gained victory over Banu Kinda, put their young to the sword, enslave their children, this should be executed if you attain victory over them by means of the power of the sword and they surrender on condition that decision rests with my discretion. If peace is concluded before the receipt of the letter it can be accepted on condition that they should all be exiled from the land; I do not want that the renegades in Islam should remain at home in their land. I wish that they should realize the consequences of their misconduct and taste a bit of their misdeeds."

(*Tabari*)

(28)

TO MUHAJIR BIN ABI UMAYYAH (R.A.A.)

This letter relates the facts about the marriage of Asma, a daughter of the famous Kindi Chief Nu'man bin Jaun with Ikrima, There seems some ambiguity and mis-understanding about it, whether she was actually married to the Prophet of Allah (S.A.W.) or not. She was one of the most beautiful women of Arabia, whose father Nu'man wanted to give her in marriage to Prophet (S.A.W.). After the consummation of marriage of Ikrima (R.A.A.) with Asma, the subject became debatable among the Companions of the Prophet of Allah (S.A.W.), whether she was daughter or sister of Nu'man and that the Prophet of Allah (S.A.W.) had actually married her or not. The matter was referred to the Caliph of the Prophet of Islam who replied as under:

"The father of Asma, Nu'man bin Jaun, visited the Prophet of Allah (S.A.W.) and paid eloquent tributes to the glamour, glory and beauty of his daughter so much so that the Holy Prophet was compelled to say to bring Asma to her home (in the vicinity of Madina). When Nu'man brought her to Madina, her father said to Prophet, "Another quality of Asma is that she never fell ill." The Prophet of Allah (S.A.W.) replied, "Had she been good in the estimation of Allah, she must have been ill . . ." the Prophet of Allah (S.A.W.) turned, away his face from her, you also do the same.'

(*Isaba*, Vol. III, P. 560).

(29)

TO MUHAJIR BIN UMAYYAH (R.A.A.)

Banu Kinda had suffered a crushing defeat at the

hands of the Muslims in the battle of Bukhair. Several families among them had been dislocated, many of them had been slain in the battle and their position had been weakened, their power had been broken and unable to take arms against the Muslims, so they tried to give vent to their feelings by filthy means. They sent two singers at different times, one of them sang verses insulting the Prophet of Allah (S.A.W.) and the other derogated the Muslims in general. Muhajir (R.A.A.) ordered that the hands of the first one were to be cut off and the front teeth of the other were extracted. Hadrat Abu Bakr (R.A.A.) was apprised of the incident, who despatched the following:

"I have come to know of the punishment you have given to the woman who had insulted the Prophet of Allah (S.A.W.). If you had not given the punishment already, surely I would have ordered her execution. The punishment awarded for a crime against the Prophet (S.A.W.) cannot be equal to the punishment awarded for a crime against ordinary public. If a Muslim insults and derogates the Prophet (S.A.W.), he will be awarded punishment meant for an apostate, while a covenanter breaks the covenant, he has declared war against the Muslims. "

(*Saff bin Umar, Tabari* P. 277).

(30)

TO THE COMMANDERS OF THE AREA OF APOSTATES

When the power of the apostates in Umman, Yaman, Hadharamaut etc. was broken and the Islamic prestige was restored, acute need was felt for the staff to administer those areas. The problem was to whom the government service was to be entrusted and who were to represent the different tribes. So the Caliph (R.A.A.) formulated a general policy, and sent the following despatch to all the commanders stationed in the areas of the apostates:

'I consider those proper for government service, who have neither been renegades themselves nor have any connection with the apostates. All of you should act upto it; only such persons should be your favourites to receive high posts. Permission should be accorded to those Muslims in the army who desire to return home; no help to fight against the enemy should be taken from the Arabs who had been apostates in the past."

(*Tabari Vol. III, P. 276*).

(31)

TO KHALID BIN WALEED (R.A.A.)

This letter has been written after the suppression of the apostate's in Islam, when their settlements were taken under Muslim army control. Abu Bakr (R.A.A.) wrote to Khalid bin Waleed (R.A.A.).

"Permission may be given to the Muslims to return to their homes. If someone desires to stay with you let him do so but none should be forced to stay on. None should be forced to fight, and render military service against his will. The tribes of Banu Tamim, Banu Qais, and Bikr bin Wail, residing in your vicinity, may be invited to cultivate the land left by Yamamah because the abandoned lands of the conquered belong to Allah and His Messenger (S.A.W.); whoso will cultivate a portion of it will be his."

(*Iktifa*, etc.)

CONQUEST OF IRAQ

The letters written by Abu Bakr (R.A.A.) in connection with the conquest of Iraq are a landmark in the history of Islamic polity, civilisation and culture representing political acumen and sagacity of the highest order. *Tarikh-i-Tabari* and *Futuhush Sham* are the main source of these letters. When Khalid bin Waleed (R.A.A.) conquered Yamamah, the first Caliph of the Prophet of Islam (S.A.W.) Abu Bakr (R.A.A.) wrote to him:

(32)

TO KHALID BIN WALEED (R.A.A.)

"I appoint you Supreme Commander of the forces of Islam for the conquest of Iraq. Raise an army from those who are steadfast in Islam. Wage war against the apostates from among the tribes of Tameem, Qais, Asad, Bikr bin Wail and Abdul Qaees who come on your way from Yamamah to Iraq. Having dealt with them, march towards Faris (Iraq) and pray to God for your victory. Having entered Iraq, conquer the port, Ubullah — the gateway to India. Try to win over the Persians and those who are their subjects so that they accept Islam or at least abandon their opposition towards it. If an excess is committed by you, give full opportunity to the injured to take his full right from you.

You belong to a nation (Ummah) who has been sent to guide the people on the right path. We pray to Almighty Allah that whomsoever He admits into our polity, they may become the best models in Islam. If, by the Grace of God, you achieve victory in Ubullah, march on towards upper Iraq and join hands with 'Ayaz bin Ghanam."

(*Iktifa*, etc.)

(33)

TO 'IYAZ BIN GHANAM

This despatch is to be studied with reference to its contents. Previously Hadrat Abu Bakr (R.A.A.) had asked Khalid bin Walid to march towards Iraq and simultaneously ordered 'Iyaz bin Ghanam (R.A.A.) to proceed to Musayyakh, conquering the Arab Chrisitan settlements on the way and reach Heerah, a crucial point for the conquest of Madain, capital of the Iranian Empire. This expedition was intended to be entrusted to the Commander who failed to reach the target of Hira in the first instance. Ayaz bin Ghanam (R.A.A.) was instructed by the Caliph of the Prophet, Abu Bakr (R.A.A.) in the following terms:

"Go to Musayyakh along with your army, concentrate your full attention to its conquest, after that enter upper Iraq, subduing the rural settlements on the way including the strategic points and march on towards Iraq so that you may join with Khalid bin Waleed (R.A.A.). Those Muslims in your army desiring to go to their home lands should be allowed, and the persons who do not want to participate in the battle in their anxiety to return to their home land, may not be allowed to render military service."

(*Saif bin Umar*, etc.)

(34)

TO KAHLID BIN WALEED AND 'IYAZ BIN GHANAM (R.A.A.)

'Those who have fought against the apsotates and remained steadfast in Islam since the demise of the Prophet of Allah (S.A.W.), invite them to participate in the war. Till further orders, none should be allowed to partake in warfare who had been a renegade in Islam."

(*Saif bin Umar, Tabari*, Vol. 4, P. 4)

(35)

TO KHALID BIN WALEED (R.A.A.) 'IYAZ BIN GHANAM (R.A.A.)

"Fear Almighty Allah, and pray to Him for help and success. Prefer the success of the Hereafter to the mundane one. The obedient to God will attain felicity in this world as well as the Hereafter. If you prefer this world to the hereafter, you will be defeated by the worldly forces, the disobedient to God will be deprived of the success of this world as well as the Hereafter. How infirm and mean are the insurgents in the sight of Allah.

(*Iktifa*, P. 350).

(36)

TO KHALID BIN WALEED AND 'IYAZ BIN GHANAM (R.A.A.)

The despatch under reference is the epilogue of the Campaigns for the conquest of Lower and Upper Iraq under Khalid bin Waleed (R.A.A.) and Iyaz Bin

Ghanam (R.A.A.) written by the Caliph of the Prophet of Allah (S.A.W.).

"When both of you meet in Heera, clear the Persian checkposts from further onslaught and when the Muslims have become safe from the hinder attacks, one commander amongst the two may remain in Heera to look after your representative governor and the Muslim there. And the other Commander should attack the enemy of God—the Persians in their capital, Madian, the seat of their power and glory.'

(*Saff bin Umar, Tabari* Vol. 4).

(37)

TO KHALID BIN WALEED (R.A.A.) AND HIS FORCES

In 11 A.H. Mutanna bin Hasitha started raiding the frontiers of Arab-Iraq during the apostasy movement; Hadrat Abu Bakr (R.A.A.), realizing the gravity of the situation encouraged him to continue his struggle against the Persians and appointed him as the Chief of the tribe and Commander of the forces. Encouraged by The Caliph of the Prophet of Allah (S.A.W.), Muthanna bin Haritha intensified his raids against Ubullah, the famous port for the merchandise of China, India, Iraq and Persia. It is at this critical juncture that the Persian Emperor intervened at the impending danger and Mutanna bin Haritha requested the Caliph Abu Bakr (R.A.A.) to send enforcement for help, which was readily accepted as Khalid bin Walid (R.A.A.) was appointed the supreme Commander of the Muslim forces in Iraq and despatched the following:

In the name of Allah, All Compassionate and Most Merciful

Peace and Blessings be upon Khalid Bin Waleed (R.A.A.) his Companions from Abdullah Abu Bakr and the Caliph of the Prophet of Allah (S.A.W.). I praise Allah, the Exalted, except Whom there is none worthy of worship. Praise be to Allah, Who has fulfilled His Promise and helped His Deen, who has bestowed Power and respect to His loyal believers, Who turned down his enemies, and over-powered all Alone over the combined forces. No doubt, there is none worthy of worship except the One.

> "Allah hath promised such of you as believe and do good works that He will surely make them to succeed (the present rulers) in the earth even as He caused those who were before them to succeed (others), and that He will surely establish for them their religion which He hath approved for them, and will give them in exchange safety after their fear. They serve Me. Those who disbelieve henceforth, they are the miscreants."
>
> (*Al-Quran*, 24:55)

This is the confirmed promise without the least possible doubt. Allah has enjoined Jehad (Striving including warfare in the way of Allah) on believers. Allah, the Supreme and Most Dignified says:

> "Warfare is ordained for you, though it is hateful unto you, but it may happen that ye hate a thing which is good for you, and it may happen that ye love a thing which is had for you. Allah knoweth, ye know not."
>
> (2:216)

Pray to Allah to fulfil His Promise that was given by Him and comply with the duty entrusted to you and thus obey Allah, the Great. The hardships, toils, turmoils, and troubles borne on this account are nothing in comparison to the attainment of the felicity of Almighty Allah, though how much great may be their financial and physical sacrifices. We have been told by the greatest certified attestator, the Prophet of Allah (S.A.W.), on whom Peace and Blessing of Allah ever shower, that on the Day of Resurrection, the martyrs will be raised with swords drawn and whatever they will entreat, Almighty Allah will give them out of gratitude they will wish to return unto this world so that their bodies may be cut into pieces. They will get all what they desire. They will be blessed with bounties from Allah which they could never imagine. What can be the highest desire of the martyrs that they may be returned to this world after their admittance into Paradise. Allah have mercy on you. Go out for Jihad whether armed or without arms and strive in the way of Allah with your body and money. There is goodness and blessing for you, if you have rightly understood true virtue. I have ordered Khalid bin Walid (R.A.A.) to go to Iraq, and stay on till the issuance of my next order. Go along with him and do not hesitate in the least. There is abundant reward from Allah for those who sincerely fight in the way of Allah and fulfil this noble task till its completion. You remain in Iraq till the receipt of my next order. Allah may bring to their successful completion all our important affairs both of this world and the Hereafter. Peace and Blessings of Allah be upon you.'

(*Futah-Ush-sham*)

(38)

TO MAZ'UR BIN 'ADI

Maz'ur Bin 'Abdi was the chief of Bani 'Ijl who was fighting against the Persians on the Arab-Iraq border. Among others were Harmala bin Muraita and Salma bin Qaim (R.A.A.) reported to be the Companions of the Prophet of Allah (S.A.W.). They were independent chieftains of their respective tribes and localities who were a menace to the Persians. Muthanna was the main protagonist for Jehad against the Persians. The following letter from Maz'ur bin 'Adi is a request made to Abu Bakr (R.A.A.) to permit him to continue jihad in the Persian territory:

"I belong to the Arab tribe of Banu 'Ijl known for their valour and horsemanship. The brave of the tribe are with me. I am a man of war fare and every one of my followers can outnumber one hundred persons from the other side. I am fully conversant with the itinerary and geographical conditions of the Persian territory. Kindly do appoint me Wali (governor) of the cultivated, green Persian-Iraq. I will conquer it on your behalf."

(*Futuh-ush-Sham*, P. 53).

THE REPLY FROM THE CALIPH

"I am in receipt of your letter and have perused its contents. Whatever you have written about yourself is perfectly true, and there are great qualities of valour and conduct in your tribe. I am of the opinion that you join with Khalid bin Walid (R.A.A.). As long as he remains in Iraq, you stay on with him. When he leaves for the next front, you accompany him."

Simultaneously Hadrat Abu Bakr (R.A.A.) sent the following reply to the complaint sent by Mutanna:

(39)

In the name of Allah, All Compassionate and Most Merciful

"Be it known to you that your compatriot 'Ijli had written to me a letter containing certain requests. I have replied to him that he should remain with the army of Khalid bin Walid (R.A.A.) till the receipt of my next orders and the same I repeat for you that you should remain in Iraq till Khalid bin Walid stays there. When he leaves for another front you should stick to your previous position You deserve all favours and promotion. Peace and blessings of Allah be upon you."

(*Futuh-ush-Sham* P. 53).

CONQUESTS IN SYRIA

Abu Bakr (R.A.A.), Caliph of the Prophet of Allah (S.A.W.) believed in the prophecies of his master, the Messenger of Allah (S.A.W.) explicitly. One of them was the good tidings of the treasures of the Qaiser and Kisra falling into the hands of the Muslims; the establishment of three Muslim army's strongholds in Syria, Iraq and Yaman and consequently the eradication of extreme poverty among the Muslims. On the face of it, these prophecies were like unbelievable fantacies, because the position of the Roman and the Persian Emperors was considered to be impregnable at that time. But the Prophet of Allah (S.A.W.) declared them to be a living reality on the basis of his prophetic insight. So the Caliph Abu Bakr (R.A.A.) declared his resolute determination to conquer Syria in the interest of Jehad and the propagation of Islam. A Session of Majlis-e-Shoora was held and the whole plan for the conquest of Syria came under discussion. The Companions were unanimous in this regard. After this a public meeting was conducted for purposes of recruitment. It did not produce the desired effect due to terror and fear of the Romans over the Arabs. So Hadrat Umar (R.A.A.) stood up and stirred up the Arabs and appealed to their sense of honour and Jehad. Consequently one of the Quraish leaders, Khalid bin Saeed, declared his willingness to participate in the Jihad along with his followers. Others followed suit. The Caliph appointed other generals for the task ahead, amongst them the most famous were (Yazid bin Abu Sufian, Abu Obaidah bin Jarrah and Shuraihbeel bin Hasana). But the speed of genetal recruitment was not very fast. After proper consultations the Muslims in Yemen were invited to participate in the incoming Syrian Jehad. So the following letter was written by the Caliph to the Muslims of Yaman:

(40)

TO THE MUSLIMS OF YAMAN

In the name of Allah, All Compassionate and Most Merciful

"The letter is intended to the address of all Yamani believers in Islam who accepted its obligations. Peace and blessings of Allah be upon them. I am grateful to Almighty Allah, except Whom there is none worthy of worship. Let it be crystal clear that Allah, the Almighty, has ordained Jehad upon all believers whether on foot or on carrier, Who has commanded them to strive in the way of Allah (Jehad) with their lives and wealth. This is an essential injunction from God and there is great reward in the sight of Allah. Here we have invited the Muslims to carry on Jehad against the Romans in Syria. They accepted the invitation with fervour and open heart, assembled in the camp and went to fight, saturated with the real spirit to make Jehad and possessed a burning desire in their hearts for the welfare in this world and the reward of the hereafter. Oh Servants of Allah! You also participate in the Jehad with those who have gone ahead, provided you have true feeling for it as you are bound to be benefitted either with the booty of warfare or martyrdom Allah, the Supreme, does not demand only lip-service but practical obedience. He will not leave His enemies till they accept and conform to the 'True Way' of life or be dependent on the Muslims ready to pay Jizya. Allah may help and protect your religion, and guide your hearts on the right channels, and cleanse your action from all evils and may reward you of the blessings of Mujahideen and those who hold steadfast. And was Salam-o-Alaikum ! "

(*Futuh-ush-Sham*).

(41)

TO KHALID BIN SAEED (R.A.A.)

Khalid bin Saeed (R.A.A.) was the first to declare his willingness to proceed for Jehad in Syria on the appeal of Abu Bakr, and Umar (R.A.A.). He was fifth among the male Muslims to accept Islam. A trusted lieutenant of the Prophet of Islam (S.A.W.) in Yaman who had returned to Madina due to disturbance there after the demise of the Prophet of Islam (S.A.W.). All the time on return to Madina, he was clad in silken clothes. Omar Farooq (R.A.A.) reprimanded him while Ali (R.A.A.) did not say anything. The misunderstanding was natural. The Caliph of the Prophet (S.A.W.) Abu Bakr (R.A.A.) willingly connived at the short-coming of Khalid bin Saeed and intended to appoint him Supreme Commander of the forces for the conquest of Syria. In the first instance, he was commissioned to proceed to Tima, a famous green spot in the desert near the Syrian frontier situated on the road leading to Damascus from Madina, the intention to establish a military base for the recruitment against Syria. As soon as the Ghassani Christian chiefs apprised the Romans of the local situation, they were commanded from their Centre to teach a lesson to Khalid bin Saeed, who informed the Caliph, Abu Bakr (R.A.A.) of the latest developments.

The Caliph commanded: "Do not retreat back on account of fear. March on bravely with your high spirits and pray to Allah for help and victory."

Khalid bin Saeed obeyed the order: In the meantime fresh reinforcement under 'Ikrima bin Abi Jehl, Waleed bin Aqabah, and Zul-Kala, a Yamani chief, reached there from Madina, carrying on their raids upon the Christians. Other Arab Chiefs, who joined hands with Khalid bin Saeed as they were unhappy with their Roman masters. Khalid informed the Caliph of the pleasant position who wrote the following:

(42)

"Continue your march cautiously, do not go too far across the boarder of Syria lest the enemy may fall upon you from the back."

(43)

Meanwhile Abu Bakr (R.A.A.) was busy collecting further reinforcements for different fronts of the Syrian Campaign. Khalid bin Saeed, in his desire to proceed further, went too far into the Syrian territory till he was encircled by the enemy and his son alongwith a number of army personnel fell into the hands of the Syrians and were killed in action. As soon as Caliph Abu Bakr (R.A.A.) came to know of the gravity of the situation, he wrote the following letter to Khalid bin Saeed.

"Remain where you (meaning thereby not to return to Madina so that people may not be discouraged there). By my life, you are as you are fast in receding your steps as quick in marching forward against the enemy. You run away from the battlefield when confronted with difficulties, you do not face the enemy resolutely till victory."

(*Tabari*, Vol. 4, P. 28, 31)

(44)

TO 'AMR BIN AL-'AAS (R.A.A.)

Due to the discomfiture of Khalid bin Saeed (R.A.A.), the resolute determination of Caliph Abu Bakr (R.A.A.) was further intensified and started a regular campaign for recruitment for the reinforcement of the army under Khalid bin Saeed. It was at this time that the discerning eye of Abu Bakr (R.A.A.) fell upon 'Amr bin Al'Aas (R.A.A.), who was well conversant with the geographical conditions of Syria as he had already travelled the country and knew its itinerary. But Abu Bakr (R.A.A.) felt hesitant to appoint him as Supreme Commander of the Syrian forces due to his previous Commitments as he was acting as Collector of Zakat in some villages of Arabia on the orders of the Prophet of Allah (S.A.W.). So instead of directing him to do so, Caliph Abu Bakr (R.A.A.) requested him in the following terms:

'While complying with the promise of the Prophet of Allah (S.A.W.) I had reappointed you on the post that was given to you by the Prophet of Allah (S.A.W.) and while sending you to Oman the Prophet of Allah (S.A.W.) had reassured you to do so. Now once again you are on the same desired job. O Abu Abdullah! I want to entrust you a job that will be more virtuous and beneficial than the present one, both in this world and the hereafter; unless the present job may appear to you so pleasant that you decline to leave it."

(45)

TO'AMR BIN AL-'AAS

So, on the Syrian front 'Amr bin al'Aas was the first and Supreme in Command, Yazid bin Abi Sufyan in Jordan, Shuraihbeel bin Hasana in the fertile middle Hooran and Abu Obaidah bin Jarrah for Damascus, Tazaruq, the real brother of Hiriqil (Heraclins), the Syrian king, was busy collecting the army to turn out Amr bin 'Aas from Palestine, who apprised the Caliph of the exact situation in the area and requested for further reinforcements. The Caliph replied as under:

"Peace and blessings of Allah be upon you. I am in receipt

of your letter in which you have made a mention of the arrival of the huge Roman forces. Let it be known to you that Al-Mighty Allah did not bestow victory upon the Prophet of Allah (S.A.W) due to large armies. When we went with the Prophet of Allah (S.A.W.) to fight against the enemy we had sometimes only 2 horses and camels in such scarcity that we could ride on them in turn. In the battle of Uhd, we had only one horse on which the Prophet of Allah (S.A.W.) rode. In spite of this, Allah helped us and granted victory over the enemies. O'Amr! Do remember well that the most obedient servant of Allah is one who is far away from evil deed, and sins. So you obey the commandments of Allah (i.e. wage Jehad with patience and steadfastness) and also enjoin upon your companions to act upon it."

(*Kanzul-Ummal, Muttaqi Burhanpuri*, Hyderabad, India Vol. 3, P. 135.)

Simultaneously, the Caliph arranged for further reinforcements for the army of 'Amr bin al'Aas and also made a resolute determination to send Khalid bin Walid (R.A.A.) and wrote to 'Amr bin al'Aas:

(46)

I have written to Khalid bin Waleed to come to your rescue. The moment he comes to you, show all kindness, treat him well and do not show arrogance in the least; although you will be Supreme in Command but do not act without his consultation. It will be better if you seek the advice of all and do not take any step without their consent."

(*Kanzal Ummal*, Vol. 3,P. 123).

(47)

TO ALL THE MILITARY COMMANDERS

'Amr bin al'Aas (R.A.A.) had capitulated the entire country across the border that was inhabited by Arabs even before the arrival of supplies from Madina and Khalid bin Walid. The defeated Roman General was chased by Yazid bin Abu Sufyan, who also defeated another army that was marching on towards the Muslims. The Romans were defeated in the battle, their leader was slain, whose chopped off head was despatched to Madina. The Caliph (R.A.A.) did not appreciate this action with approbation, on the contrary, wrote the following despatch to all the military commanders:

"Do not send me the cut off heads. Despatches in news are sufficient."

(*Sharah As-Sear-al-Kabeer, Sarakhsi*, Dairatul M'aarif, Hyderabad. Ind. Vol. 1, P. 78).

(48)

TO'AMR BIN AL 'AAS (R.A.A.)

The despatch bears no reference and context, possibly may be a portion of a letter sent to Amr bin al'Aas by the Caliph (R.A.A.)

"Be it clear to you that beware, you know well the will of the Prophet of Allah'u (S.A.W.) about Ansar that listen to the virtuous amongst them and connive at their faults."

(*Kanzul Ummal*, Vol. 2, P. 163).

(49)

Similarly in another despatch the Caliph (R.A.A.) is reported to have addressed 'Amr bin Al'Aas in the following words.

"The Prophet of Allah (S.A.W.) used to consult us in matters of warfare, you also do the same;"

(*Kanzul 'Ummaal*, Vol. 2, P. 163).

(50)

TO THE MILITARY COMMANDERS

The conquest of Syria is a unique phenomenon in the history of Islam during the reign of the first Caliph, Abu Bakr (R.A.A.). Considering the pomp and glory, material strength of the Romans in men and money, the conquest seems to be almost incredulous. When news of the collection of the Roman army, numbering about 2 hundred thousand men, reached the Caliph (R.A.A.), it was decided that the Muslims should face the enemy jointly in a combined way i.e. all the Muslim soldiers under the four generals should attack the enemy together and each general should lead the five times daily prayers of their respective contingents separately. The Caliph (R.A.A.) sent the following despatch to face the hard, rugged practical front of the battle with a cheerful heart as the Muslims are the soldiers of Allah and they are bound to succeed, if they remain virtuous:

"You all join together and be one army and face the armies of the infidel. You are true to Allah, in fidelity and steadfastness. Surely Allah will help the faithful in their hour of need and will leave the rebels in wildness. The only reason for the discomfiture of ten thousand faithful men against the same number or more of enemy can be their misdeeds. So shun the evil. All the commanders should assemble with their men in Yarmouk. ' Every Commander should lead the prayers of his respective army."

(51)

TO KHALID BIN WALEED (R.A.A.)

All the Muslim generals assembled together in a plain near the valley of Yarmouk and the Romans selected a place of their own choice that proved to be their doom. Realizing the gravity of the situation, the Caliph Abu Bakr (R.A.A.) felt that the Muslim army needed a general who could infuse courage and kindle their hearts with confidence, self-reliance based on the trust of Almighty Allah. So he despatched the following message to Khalid bin Walid, who was returning to Heera after reaching the frontiers of Syria and Mesopotamia.

"You move at once and join the Muslim forces in Yarmouk. The Muslim army feels grieved at the presence of the Romans just as the Romans do. Beware! You do not repeat the mistake committed by you. By the Grace of God, none can inflict such grievous injuries on the enemy as you can, and none among the Muslims can kindle the hearts of the Muslim army with confidence and encourage except you. O Abu Sulaiman! I pray that Allah, the Supreme, may Grace you with the passion of Jehad, and you may be blessed with Divine Blessings. Let your zeal for Jehad may reach its completion, so Allah will bestow His Reward in full. Let pride for pelf and power never enter into your heart otherwise your good-deeds shall come to naught and God's Help shall be withdrawn from your side. Do not entirely rely on your planning because success is dependent upon the Grace of Allah, the Supreme, and not upon human endeavours. Reward for every good or bad action lies with Him alone." (*Tabari*, Vol. 4, P. 46)

POLICY DIRECTIVES TO THE MILITARY COMMANDERS:

1. After the conquest of Syria, brisk trade activities between Arabia and Syria started, so the Caliph wrote the following letter to the Syrian governors.

"You have reached a country where business with interest is rampant, so it is essential that if you buy silver or gold with the same coins, both of them should be equal in weight. Similarly if you buy corn, it should be sold with equal weight with which you purchased it."

(*Kanzul Ummaal* Vol. 2, P. 231)

This is considered to be landmark in the history of commercial activity of Islamic state.

Various directives issued to different commanders from the Caliph (R.A.A.) heightens the respect, prestige, personality and estimate of the first Caliph of Islam. In this connection some of the guidelines provided by the Caliph Abu Bakr (R.A.A.) are reproduced to form a correct estimate of his personality .

2. The first piece of advice given to the first commander of Syria, Yazid bin Abu Sufyan, while bidding farewell from Madina for Syria.

"Yazid, My advice is to fear Allah always, obey Him, prefer His pleasure. If Allah grants you victory in the battlefield against the enemy, do not put ignorant round the neck of any one, enchain them not round their feet, do not cut or disfigure their bodies, do not deceive the enemy or show treachery in the warfare, do not show cowardice, do not kill the children or the women and the infirm old persons, do not cut any fruit-bearing tree, nor destroy the date trees, nor cut the jegular vein of an animal unless it be necessary for provision of food. You will come across the persons who will be busy with prayers in their monasteries, and thus leading monastic life, do not interfere with them. And you will come across the persons on whose heads Satan had drawn the hair cut into two, if they refuse to accept Islam or do not agree to pay Jiziya to come under the protection of Islam, chop off their heads into two. Do remember that Allah, the Supreme, do help those who make sacrifice for Him and His Prophet (S.A.W.). You are my first in commander (in Syria), I have made you incharge of many respectable Muslims, so treat them well, safeguard their honour and rights, show kindness and goodness to them and also consult them in your affairs."

(Futuh-ush-Sham)

3. When the next Commander of the forces of Islam, Abu Obaidah bin Jarrah (R.A.A.) completed his preparations for the march, Abu Bakr (R.A.A.) came to see him and said:

"Do listen to me with rapt attention. There are a number of respectable people of high pedigree, men of virtue, apt in the art of horsemanship, used to fight for personal name, honour and valour, today they are going to fight with the sincere desire and true passion for the pleasure of Allah and His Blessings. Do behave with them nicely and show good treatment to all. The people must be equal before you in the matter of rights and dispensation of justice." (*Futuh-ush-Sham*)

4. Qais bin Hubaira Makshooh Muradi (R.A.A.), formerly Commander-in-Chief of the forces of Aswad-i-'Ansi, (the apostate) commanding influence over many Yamani tribes, a veteran warrior with wide experience in warfare had come to Madina at the invitation of Abu Bakr (R.A.A.) to partake in the Syrian campaign under Abu Obaidah bin Jarrah (R.A.A.). He was a leading personality of Yaman, commanding high respect. He was commended by Caliph Abu Bakr (R.A.A.) to Abu Obaidah bin Jarrah (R.A.A.) in the following words:

A great Arab personality of high esteem, reputed in the art of horsemanship and bravery (warrior) is accompanying you whom the Muslims cannot afford to ignore either in actual battle or matters relating to warfare. Make him your close adviser, treat him extremely well, impress upon him that you need him most and are considerate to him to the utmost. This type of treatment and behaviour will make him your well-wisher and he will fight for you in the true spirit against your enemy."

(*Futuh-ush-Sham*)

5. On the other hand, Caliph Abu Bakr (R.A.A.) advise Qais bin Hubairah about Abu Obaidah bin Jarrah (R.A.A.) as following:

"I am sending you with Abu Obaidah (R.A.A.) who is known by the title 'Amin' i.e. the Trustworthy. He bears the excesses done by others but does not commit cruelty himself if someone maltreats him, he excuses; if some cuts adrift from him, he restores that cut off relationship. He is very kind to the Muslims, very strict with the non-believers. Do not disobey or deviate from him who will not ask you to do something devoid of goodness. I have reminded him to listen to you, and act upto your advice. Whatever advice you offer him, fear of Allah should be engrained into it. During the days of Jahiliyah, we used to hear your capabilities of prowess and bravery for the preponderance of Islam and against the infidels. Allah will reward you handsomely for this service to Islam."

(*Futuh-ush-Sham*)

6. Khalid bin Saeed bin 'Aas (R.A.A.) was advised by the Caliph (R.A.A.), while bidding him farewell to the frontiers of Syria:

"You have given me advices which I keep very dear to my heart. Now I desire to provide you with certain guidelines that you may attend to them and act accordingly. You are the old veteran of Islam and its ardent worker and this station in life is very high in this regard. People took to you for guidance and action. You are going to participate in the Syrian campaign for Jehad, whose reward is very high in the estimation of Allah. I fervently hope that you have determined to part with your life in a sincere manner or the pleasure of Allah and His Reward. Your conduct should be to keep the 'Scholars of Deen' steadfast, the ignorant may take interest in the affairs of Deen and become its followers with constant advice and vigilance. Be the best well-wishers of the Muslims, advise the Commander-in-Chief of Islam in a manner that the general good of the people may prevail, and the truth may become supreme. Every action of yours should be for the pleasure and glory of God under the strict sense of control as if you are seeing Him. Consider yourself among the dead soon, death will overtake us, we will be resurrected, and our actions will be accounted for. Allah Ta'aala may grant us strength and guidance to glorify His praises and blessings bestowed upon us and be in constant fear of his punishment."

(*Futuh-ush-Sham*)

LETTERS TO COMMANDERS IN SYRIA

At the time of Syrian expedition several factors helped the Muslims. The Muslim attitude of good behaviour and factious conditions of the Christian nobility in Syria. The Christian religious fanaticism had divided them into two different strata of society—the haves and the have nots—the one was extremely wealthy and the other the down trodden. The result was that the general public became disgusted and the Muslim opposition was lessened to a great extent. The Christian chiefs lost their courage and their opposition was lowered down to a great extent. The Syrian expedition started in 13 A.H. It took about six years and there were several expeditions against them — namely the important ones, the battle of Ajnadain and the battle of Yarmauk.

The conquest of Syria had become part and parcel of Muslims' belief because the Prophet of Allah (S.A.W.) had prophesied its conquest. The Muslims believed it as predestined. The Qaisar (Roman emperor) proclaimed emergency and sent urgent despatches to other Christian chiefs both Arabs and Romans, and delivered the following speech:

"O believers in the Christian faith! God was very kind to you. He granted preponderance to your faith over Persians, Turks and over many other nations. Who gave respect and honour to you — Main reason being that you acted upto the injunctions of the Book of your Cherisher (rabh) and were abiding by your Prophet's actions. When you deviated from the right path, your image became loose and the Arabs were encouraged to attack upon you. By God, I always ignored them and did not consider them worthy of any consideration and never apprehended that we will be put to test to fight against them. Bare-headed, ill-dressed, hungry and down-trodden on account of their barren lands and poverty, they were forced to come out of their land to attack upon you. You also come out to face them to protect your faith, country, women and children. I am on the way to proceed further, will arrange to send an army comprising of horsemen and men on foot. I have appointed military commanders for you, so obey them."

The Roman Emperor proceeded to Palestine to make the necessary preparations and visited all the important military headquarters — Hims — Antakia etc. He took the supreme command of the battle into his own hands and sent messengers for help in men and weapons to Mesopotamia, Asia Minor, Arminea and other provinces.

During this period the military commanders appointed by Hadrat Abu Bakr (R.A.A.) had entered Syria, and engaged themselves into several skirmishes. Abu Obaidah bin Jarrah (R.A.A.) conquered the important military cantonment at Jabiya. The local intelligence under Abu Obaidah informed him that the Roman Emperor was visiting all the important cantonment collecting 'Such large army that was never accomplished by his forefathers or any other ruler.' Abu Obaidah despatched the following letter to the Caliph Abu Bakr (R.A.A.).

Information has been received by me that the Roman Emperor, Herarclius, has encamped in Antakia, called for armies outside Syria which are about to reach to fight with the Muslims. This is just to inform you to do the necessary needful action."

(*Futuh-ush-Sham* — Azdi P. 24).

(52)

REPLY TO ABU OBAIDAH BIN JARRAH (R.A.A)

In the name of Allah, All Compassionate and Most Merciful

I am in receipt of your letter informing me about the military preparation of the Roman Emperor, whose encamping in Antakia necessary means that he along with his army will be defeated and the Muslims will be victorious by the Grace of Allah. You have stated that he has arranged to collect his militia from every quarter of his domain. This is no news to us because we know it before hand, as no nation can relinquish its rule without giving battle to the enemy. You know it too well that many Muslims had already fought against them when death was as dear to them as life itself to the enemy. The Muslim wanted to give their life for the attainment of the pleasure of Allah and felicitation of the Great Reward. They preferred Jehad (striving in every way) in the path of Allah, to the accompaniment of their chaste wives and priceless camels. A single warrior among them is better than one thousand from the infidels. Keeping this example of the valiants in Islam, fight out against the enemy regardless of the numerical strength. Allah is with you. In spite of this I shall send abundant provisions for you with which you will be satisfied, and will not covet more. Peace and Blessing of Allah be upon you."

(*Futuh-ush-Sham*).

(53)

REPLY TO YAZID BIN ABI SUFYAM (R.A.A)

Yazid bin Abu Sufyan also reported the concentration of the forces of Roman Emperor to the centre of Islam — Madina and wrote following letter to the Caliph, Abu Bakr (R.A.A.)

"Almighty Allah created fear in the heart of the Roman Emperor who left Palestine for Antakia at the news of our attack in Syria. He has appointed Roman commanders in all important and strategical cities in Syria, ordered them to fight against us. The Syrian chiefs who have communicated with us, have reported that Herarclius has also called for armies in large numbers from other domains outside Syria to fight with us with all possible military armaments. We urgently wait for your further orders in the matter."

Hadrat Abu Bakr (R.A.A.) wrote the following in reply to the above:

In the name of Allah, All Compassionate and Most Merciful

Received your letter stating that the Roman Emperor was so struck with terror on account of Muslim forces that he reached Antakia fleeing from Palestine, Damascus and Hams. When we were in company with the Prophet of Allah (S.A.W.), Almighty Allah Whom we are grateful, struck terror into the hearts of the mushrikeen on the one hand and helped us by descending the sacred Angels. The help was given to us by Allah by striking terror and fear into the rank and file of the enemy for the establishment of Deen-i-Islam. We are today inviting people to the same faith and Deen that was helped by Allah. By your Rabb! Allah will not bring the end of the Muslims like criminals. Those who declare that "there is no God except Allah, the only One," cannot be at par with those who worship God along with other deities and believe in many gods. When you encounter any of the Roman Emperor's armies, you fall upon them fearlessly, and fight with them tooth and nail. Allah, the Great, will never leave you in the lurch, and will never lift His hand from your help. Allah, the High and Exalted had informed that a small army overcomes a great army by His Grace. Anyway, I will send you the supplies and men constantly and persistently so much so that will meet all your requirements, and God willing, you will not feel deficiency even for a single person. Peace and Blessing of Allah be upon you.

(Futuh-ush-Sham)

The despatches sent by Abu Obaidah bin Jarrah (R.A.A.) and Yazid bin Abi Sufyan (R.A.A.) did not create any adverse effect upon the mind of Hadrat Abu Bakr (R.A.A.). Neither he felt fear nor there seemed any weakness in his resolute determination for the conquest of Syria as he was confident without the least doubt that the prophesy of the Prophet of Allah (S.A.W.) regarding the conquest of Syria must come true. So he accelerated his efforts for the recruitment and mobilisation of the Muslim army. So a powerful and impressive camp was formed in the vicinity of Madina, as tribal chiefs along with their men were pouring in from Yaman, and the Caliph Abu Bakr (R.A.A.) was sending them to the Syrian frontier, merging them into the main army. Several influential and important chiefs from Mecca had also come to Madina to join the Syrian campaign, and so Hadrat Abu Bakr (R.A.A.) with his far-sighted erudition and inward insight appointed 'Amr bin al'Aas (R.A.A.) to look after the army at Jabia. 'Amr bin al'Aas (R.A.A.) was a highly responsible personality, well conversant with geographical position of the area, fully armed with political acumen of the time and force of circumstances whose arrival greatly encouraged the Muslim forces there.

(54)

TO ABU OBAIDAH BIN JARRAH (R.A.A.)

The news of the Muslim reinforcements from Madina to the commanders in Syria spread like wild fire, and the informers sent exaggerated news of the numerical strength and panic prevailed in the military circles of the enemy. Immediately envoys were sent to the Roman

Emperor for succour in men and provision who sent the encouraging reply with the following last words:

"I will send armies in such number that earth will be incapacitated to accommodate them." The Muslims were under the impression that they had to fight with the local Syrian army only but they felt a little bit hesitant when they came to know that they had to deal with the forces of Asia Minor, Armenia and Turkey also. So their Commander in Chief, Abu Obaidah (R.A.A.) sent the following report to the centre:

Informers brought the news that the scouts of the forces from outside Syria have arrived and the commanders of the big cities have sent messages to the Roman Emperor for help in provision. Roman Emperor has written to his commanders.

"The population of one of your big cities is larger than the whole Arab Army. Do not fear, face the enemy openly, suppliesare in abundance from the rear."

The news are also pouring in that the Muslims feel apprehensive to fight.

(*Futuh-ush-Sham*, P. 37).

Abu Bakr (R.A.A.) the Caliph of the prophet of Allah (S.A.W.) replied as under.

In the name of Allah, All Compassionate and Most Merciful

"Your letter has been received stating therein that the armies of the enemy have been sent to fight with you. It also indicates that the Roman Emperor has promised to send as large an army that it would be difficult to accommodate it on the surface of this earth. By God! By your very presence there, the earth has been straitened to them in spite of its vastness By Allah! I am confident that you will soon expel the Roman

Emperor Some Antakia where he is staying at present. You spread your contingent armies throughout the villages, inhabited agricultural lands. Deprive the local Syrian army of food and fodder, thus making their life extremely miserable for them. Do not besiege large cities till the receipt of my further orders. If the enemy advances towards you for fighting, you also do the same and pray to God that He may grant you power over the enemy. I will send double or equal quantity of provision to you as the enemy receives. Gratitude is due to Almighty God that neither you are less in number nor weak in strength. I do not know why do you hesitate to fight against them. I am sure Allah, the Great will grant you victory and power over the enemy. He wants to see how you offer thanks to Him when you have the upper hand over the enemy. Behave very nicely with 'Amr bin al'Aas, who has been advised by me never to hesitate to tender you good advice and right course of action. He is a man of mature experience and sound opinion. And Peace and Blessings of Allah be upon you."

(*Futuh-ush-Sham*).

(55)

TO KHALID BIN WALEED (R.A.A)

The battle of Ajnadain is one of the landmarks in the history of Islam. The Roman Emperor had mustered up his forces not only from the Syrian soil but from all parts of his empire. Naturally the Muslims were apprehensive, especially when they had adverse experience in the skirmishes at Mauta and the defeat of the son of Khalid bin Saeed at Marajus-Suffar (southern portion of Syria). The spirit of the Romans ran high, and they proudly declared, "By God, we shall teach a lesson to Abu Bakr that he will forget to think to attack us." After this they started preparations on a large scale with a foul intention to destroy the Islamic State at Madina.

The appointment of Khalid bin Walid (R.A.A.) as the Supreme Commander of the Syrian forces encouraged Caliph Abu Bakr (R.A.A.) to declare "By Allah! I will inflict such a crushing defeat to the Romans through Khalid that all their Satanic ambitions will die away." At this time Hadrat Khalid bin Waleed was busy in subduing the chiefs on the frontiers of Iraq offering them Peace with Jiziya. At this moment the urgent call from the Caliph was received by him.

"Let it be known to you that on receipt of this letter you leave Iraq, leaving all those persons who were in Iraq before you arrived there. You shall take in company those seasoned military men who were with you in Yamamah, or had joined you on your way from Yamamah to Iraq or those who had come to you from Hijaz March towards Syria forth-with and join with Abu Obaidah's army. You will be Supreme Commander when you reach there. More Peace and Blessings of Allah be upon you."

(*Futuh-ush-Sham*, P. 5).

(56)

TO ABU OBAIDAH BIN JARRAH (R.A.A.)

In appointing Khalid bin Walid as supreme commander of the Muslim forces in Syria, Caliph Abu Bakr (R.A.A.) has solely decided the issue on merit as he had excelled all in warfare, and was par excellence in infusing confidence in others as he was the very embodiment of the same. Caliph Abu Bakr (R.A.A.) wrote the following despatch to Abu Obaidah (R.A.A.) while entrusting supreme command to Khalid bin Waleed (R.A.A.):

"Let it be known that I have entrusted to Khalid the

supreme command of the Muslim Syrian forces against the Romans. You shall not oppose but obey him and act upon his advice, knowing fully well that you are better than Khalid, I have made him your officer in this regard as I am of the view that he has better strategical sense in warfare than you. We pray to Allah, the Almighty, that we may stick to the Right Path. And Peace and Blessings of Allah be upon you."

(*Futus-ush-Shàm*, P. 74).

In 13 A.H. Rabi-ul-Awwal. Khalid bin Waleed (R.A.A.) left to take charge of the supreme command in Syria, and while leaving the frontiers of Iraq, Khalid addressed a letter to the people (Muslims) of Syria and another letter to Abu Obaidah bin Jarrah. In the first letter he addressed the Muslims thus:

"I have been appointed your Commander-in-Chief and very soon I shall meet you. Be patient and do not fear in the least. Soon the promise of Allah shall come to pass."

The other letter was addressed by Khalid bin Waleed to Abu Obaidah bin Jarrah, the veteran senior leader of the Muslim forces in Syria. One of the earliest Believers in Islam, a very close companion of the Prophet of Allah (S.A.W.) with a glorious record of services both in peace and war, he was well known for his amiable habits and good manners with a high distinction among the companions of the Prophet of Allah (S.A.W.). In view of the above stated position Khalid bin Walid almost felt shy to be the officer of Abu Obaidah bin Jarrah (R.A.A.), so he wrote the following letter to Abu Obaidah acknowledging his superiority, expressing his own humility to be the leader of the Islamic forces in Syria in the presence of such a formidable and influential personality like Abu Obaidah:

In the name of Allah, All Compassionate and Most Merciful

FROM KHALID BIN WALEED (R.A.A.)
TO ABU OBAIDAH BIN JARRAH (R.A.A.)

Peace and Blessings of Allah be upon you except Whom none is worthy of worship. I pray to Almighty Allah to save me and yourself from the Fearful Day (Day of Resurrection), punishment of hell, worldly troubles and tribulations. The Caliph of the Prophet of Allah (S.A.W.) Abu Bakr (R.A.A.) has ordered me to take charge of the command of the forces of Islam in Syria. By God, I, neither desired nor requested for this post nor had any correspondence with the Caliph (R.A.A.) on this issue. God's blessings be upon you, your esteem and status shall be the same in spite of my being the Commander-in-Chief. Your order and advice shall not be disregarded, no decision will be taken without your consultation. You are one of the most distinguished personalities of the Muslims. Neither your grand portion can be denied nor your guidance can be ignored. Prayer is to Almighty Allah that He may bring his Graces to its completion and both of us may be saved from the chastisement of the Hell. Peace and blessings of Allah be upon you."

(*Futuh-ush-Sham*, P. 62)

(57)

TO THE COMMANDERS OF THE ARMY

Expediency within the framework of Islamic Sharia (jurisprudence) is the keynote of the successful operation of Islamic Law and its all-pervading comprehensive attitude. One of the commanders of Abu Bakr (R.A.A.) wrote to know his opinion about an influential Arab Chief who had been a prisoner during one of the battles fought during the apostasy movement and wanted to be free after the payment of ransom money. Abu Bakr (R.A.A.) refused to accept the proposal as he appeared to Abu Bakr (R.A.A.) a dangerous influential man, who participated in many battles against the Muslims, inflicted heart-rending physical injuries on them. The Caliph of the Prophet (S.A.W.) considered the existence of such a person against the interests of Islam and ordered to be slain.

"The Quran has clearly laid down that when you meet in battle those who disbelieve, then it is smiting of the necks until when you have routed them, then making fast of bonds; and afterwards either grace or ransom till the war lay down its burdens." (47:4) In the battle of Badr the Prophet of Allah (S.A.W.) acted on the second portion of the verse while on another occasion the Messenger of Allah (S.A.W.) ordered one or two captives to be slain in the interest of Islam as they were inveterate mischief-mongers. The Caliph wrote: "Do not release him on ransom but kill him."

(*Kunzul Ummaal*, Vol. 1, P. 312.)

PROCLAMATION TO SUCCESSION

The first great battle of Ajnadain in Syria had come to an end, and preparations were under way for the conquest of the Syrian Capital—Damascus when Abu Bakr (R.A.A.) fell ill so seriously that all hopes of recovery were lost. At that time there were great living companions of the Prophet of Allah (S.A.W.) in the personalities of Usman Ghani (R.A.A.) Zubair bin Awwam, Talha bin Abdullah, Hadrat Ali, and Umar Farooq (R.A.A.). Of all Hadrat Umar (R.A.A.) was eminently suited for the job according to the estimate of Abu Bakr (R.A.A.) as he was his right hand companion during his short reign of two and a half years, whose erudition, constant advice and guidance was a source of great strength to the cause of Islam, who took keen interest in the matters concerning the government of the State. He was selfless, full of resolute determination and a man of practical nature. Hadrat Abu Bakr (R.A.A.) decided to appoint Umar Farooq (R.A.A.) as his successor. In the first instance he called Abdur Rahman bin Auf and asked him about Umar Farooq (R.A.A.) who replied," You know him better than me. "

Abu Bakr (R.A.A.), "In spite of this, I want to know your opinion about him."

Abdur Rahman said, "Umar is far better than you know you know him."

After this Abu Bakr called Hadrat Usman (R.A.A.) and asked his opinion about Umar (R.A.A.), who said, "What can I tell you in this regard? You are in a better position to know him than myself."

When Abu Bakr (R.A.A.) insisted to express his views about him, Hadrat Usman Ghani replied, "The internal condition of Hadrat Umar is far better than his exterior self, and he is best amongst us."

Abu Bakr (R.A.A.) said, "Blessings of Allah be upon you! If you did not give me your opinion about him, I would have appointed you as the Caliph of Islam. "

Abu Bakr (R.A.A.) also consulted other important influential companions of the Prophet of Allah (S.A.W.) regarding the nomination of Hadrat Umar (R.A.A.) who also expressed their opinion in his favour. After this some other persons also came who said to Hadrat Abu Bakr, "How will you account for the selection of Umar Farooq (R.A.A.) on the day of Judgment in spite of high rough, tough and strict attitude?" Ailing Abu Bakr (R.A.A.) became very spirited, sat down reclining and said, "You want me to make fearful of God, surely I will say that I have selected the best man as Caliph." Saying this, he laid down on his bed, called for Usman Ghani (R.A.A.), and gave the following in writing:

In the name of Allah, All Compassionate and Most Merciful

This is a proclamation from Abu Bakr bin Abi Qahafah who is stepping into the first stage of the life in the Hereafter, after just passing the last stage of this life, where reality unveils itself in such a crystal clear manner that even the non-believer has to believe, the evil-doer has to affirm in the punishment of the Hereafter, and the liar is compelled to speak out the truth. I appoint Umar bin Khattab as Caliph after my death. It is your duty to obey his orders and act according to his guidance; in selecting him I have tried my utmost to fulfil the obligations relating to Allah, His Deen, my own conscience and the welfare of the Muslims. I am fully hopeful that Umar will act according to justice and equity. But if he does not act accordingly, he will be responsible for his own actions like all other people. I have, in my own way, done my very best for the welfare of Muslims, and the unseen, affairs are beyond the purview of my knowledge. The wrong doers will have to suffer for their deeds soon. And Peace and Blessings of Allah be upon you."

(*Kanzul Ummaal*, Vol. 3, P. 145).